A Dictionary
of the
Sussex Dialect

The Barbican, Lewes Castle

A Dictionary

OF THE

Sussex Dialect

AND

Collection of Provincialisms

BY

The Rev. W. D. Parish

Vicar of Selmeston, Sussex

Augmented with material by E. V. Lucas
Illustrated by Frederick L. Griggs A.R.A.
Edited by Dick Richardson

Country Books

Published by:
Country Books
Courtyard Cottage, Little Longstone, Bakewell, Derbyshire DE45 1NN

© 2001 Country Books

ISBN 1 898941 68 8

The Dictionary by Rev. W. D. Parish
was first published in 1875 by Farncombe & Co., Lewes.

The material by E. V. Lucas is from Highways & Byways in Sussex
published by Macmillan & Co in 1904 and 1928 (pocket edition).

The illustrations are by Frederick L. Griggs A.R.A. from
Highways & Byways in Sussex
published by Macmillan & Co in 1904 and 1928 (pocket edition).

Cover illustration:
Pulborough

DEDICATION
I dedicate this edition to Tony Wales,
Man of Sussex, writer, folklorist and folksinger,
who over a period of nearly half a century
has always been helpful with advice,
and willing to share his knowledge and
love of Sussex with me.
Dick Richardson

Printed and bound by:
MFP Design & Print

CONTENTS

The Judge's House, East Grinstead

FOREWORD

William Douglas Parish was born on 16th December 1833, the son of Sir Woodbine Parish, F.R.S. Woodbine was a diplomatist and naturalist who encouraged British relations with South America, and the Treaty of Peace signed at Paris on 20th November 1815 on the conclusion of the Napoleonic War, was in his handwriting. He also discovered the fossils of the magatherium, mylodon and glytodon.

William was educated at Charterhouse, and afterwards at Trinity College, Oxford, where he gained an M.A. In 1859 he was ordained and spent four years at Firle where he served as curate, before being preferred to the vicarage of Selmeston with Alciston.

In 1866 he supervised the rebuilding of the church at Selmeston – then pronounced Simson. Each stone was marked and reset in its place. In 1877 he was appointed by Bishop Durnford Chancellor of the Cathedral of Chichester. In 1886 he was elected to the Council of the Sussex Archaeological Society, becoming its first chairman in 1895.

His other publications covered a wide field. His educational works ranged from poetry for elementary classes to a manual of instruction for the electric telegraph. He co-published a dictionary of the Kentish dialect with the Rev. W. F. Shaw and edited the Sussex Domesday for the Sussex Archaeological Society.

He died on 23rd September, 1904, and is buried in the church-yard at Selmeston.

In Buxted Park

ORIGINAL PREFACE

The march of education must sooner or later trample down and stamp out anything like distinctive provincial dialect in England; but when this result shall have been effected, much that is really valuable will be lost to our language, unless an effort is promptly made to collect and record words which, together with the ideas which first rendered them necessary, are rapidly falling into disuse.

Although in all such collections there will be a large proportion of words and phrases which are mere curiosities of expression, utterly useless to the science of language, yet there will remain a considerable number well worthy of being retained, and if possible revived.

Every year new words are being imported into the English language and gradually coming into general use amongst us. Too many of these are selected from the ghastly compounds of illiterate advertizers, and many more are of the most offensive type of slang – the sweepings of the music-hall, the leavings of the prize-ring and the worst specimens of Americanisms, selected to the exclusion of many good old English words which are to this day more frequently used in the United States of America than in our own country.

The English Dialect Society, which has lately been formed, will soon become the centre of a very valuable influence, by encouraging and uniting many word-collectors who have been quietly working for some time past in different parts of the country, and by giving a right direction to their labours.

To the Rev. W. W. Skeat, as the representative of that Society, I owe more than I am able to express for the guidance that he has given me, and the pains that he has taken to render this work as free as possible from imperfections. Without his assistance I could never have presented it to the reader in the form it now assumes.

Professor Bosworth also, although busily engaged (in his 87th year) in bringing out a new quarto Anglo-Saxon dictionary, found time to encourage me in my work, and set me in the right track by correcting the first pages of my proof. To him and many others my best thanks are due. Such a work could never have been done single-handed, and volunteers have come forward on all sides to help me.

The Rev. W. de St. Croix, late editor of the Sussex Archaeological Society's Collections, has for many years given me valuable assistance. Miss Bessie C. Curteis, of Leasam, near Rye, has contributed at least 200 words, with conversational illustrations and legends from the East Sussex district. The Rev. J. C. Egerton, of Burwash, has also placed at my disposal his collection of upwards of 100 words in use in his section of the county; and when I add that the Rev. C. Swainson has helped me in my folklore, and Mr. James Britten, of the British Museum, has corrected my botanical definitions, the reader will understand how much kindly effort has been made to render my work successful, and how little its success (if it shall be attained) is due to myself.

W. D. PARISH.

While my Dictionary was in the press, I received the following words from the Rev. A. F. Kirkpatrick, Trinity College, Cambridge and Edgar Sharpe, Esq., Carshalton. They came too late to be placed in their alphabetical order, but were too interesting to be omitted. [They are marked †.]

The following words (kindly sent to me by Frederick E. Sawyer, Esq., of Brighton), are from the Brighton "Costumal," (custumal) 1580; i.e., a book of certain customs, chiefly relating to fishing, which received Royal confirmation at that date. [They are marked §.]

LIST OF AUTHORITIES

W. Durrant Cooper's Sussex Glossary.
Halliwell's Dictionary of Archaic and Provincial Words.
W. Holloway's General Dictionary of Provincialisms.
Bosworth's Anglo-Saxon Dictionary.
Sussex Archeological Collections.
Ayscough's Shakespeare.
Brand's Popular Antiquities.
R. Chambers' Book of Days.
Notes and Queries.
M. A. Lower, Contributions to Literature, etc., etc.
Professor Leo's Treatise on the Local Nomenclature of the Anglo-
        Saxons.
Stratmann's Old English Dictionary.
Wedgwood's Dictionary of English Etymology.
Ray's Collection of Local Words.
Bosham Manor Customs, and the old books of the Manor of
Arundel (kindly lent by R. G. Raper, Esq.).
Various Inventories of Farm and Household Goods of the last
        three Centuries.

Lancing

THE SUSSEX DIALECT

In almost every establishment in the country there is to be found some old groom, or gardener, bailiff, or factotum, whose odd expressions and quaint sayings and apparently outlandish words afford a never-failing source of amusement to the older as well as to the younger members of the household, who are not aware that many of the words and expressions which raise the laugh are purer specimens of the English language than the words which are used to tell the story in which they are introduced.

Every schoolboy home for the holidays at Christmas knows that the London cabman who drives him to the theatre accentuates the word much more classically than the young gentleman who sits inside, who, if he had the audacity to pronounce theatron with a short a in his next construe at school, would send a shudder through the Form amid which he would soon find himself in a lower place. So it is with our Sussex words; they sound strange to ears that are not accustomed to them; and by some persons they may be supposed to be mere slang expressions, not worthy of attention; but when they are examined, many of them will be found to be derived from the purest sources of our language, and to contain in themselves a clear reflection of the history of the county in which they are used.

Every page of this dictionary will show how distinctly the British, Roman, Saxon and Norman elements are to be traced in the words in every day use among our labouring people, who retain among them many of the oldest forms of old words which although they have long ago become obsolete among their superiors in education, are nevertheless still worthy of our respect and attention. Like the old coins which he so often turns up with his plough, the words of the Sussex labourer bear a clear stamp of

Cowdray

days long past and gone and tell a story of their own.

The fact that I have lived for several years in a village spelt Selmeston and pronounced Simpson; within reach of Brighthelmston, pronounced Brighton, and next to the village of Chalvington, called Charnton, will, I think, be considered sufficient excuse for the direction my studies have taken. My daily intercourse with persons speaking the purest Sussex dialect has enabled me to add from time to time many fresh words to the excellent list published by Mr. Durrant Cooper in his "Glossary" (which must always be the guide book for all who take an interest in the subject); and when I found that I had added as many as a thousand words to those which he had already published, I thought I might venture to take the next step forward in making known the Sussex dialect among Sussex people by the publication of this book. I had called it a dictionary of the Sussex dialect before I was aware that my friend Mr. M. A. Lower had stated in an article published in the Sussex Archaeological Collections that there is no such thing as a Sussex dialect at all. I should be sorry to appear to set up my opinion in opposition to one whose authority on all matters connected with the antiquities of our county is so generally recognized; but I am sure that he will allow me the use of the word to indicate a form of speech, which in words and pronounciation is strictly defined by geographical boundaries, and frequently proves completely unintelligible to strangers who hear it for the first time.

So far as a distinct collection of words can be called a dialect, it may be said that there are three dialects in use in the County of Sussex, the East Sussex, Mid Sussex and West Sussex; and it will be observed that I have marked this distinction in the following pages by affixing to most of the words the initial of the district in which they are used. But besides these, there are many words which, as far as I can ascertain, are common to the whole county, and to these no distinctive letter is annexed.

I should (roughly) define the East Sussex district as the part of the county lying east of a line drawn northward from Hastings; the West Sussex district would be bounded by a line running northward from Shoreham; and the Mid Sussex district would, of course, be found between the two. I must request the reader to bear in mind these geographical distinctions, because few persons except word-collectors are acquainted with provincial expressions beyond their own district; and without this explanation it might be supposed that many words which occur in my list are not Sussex words at all.

The sources from which our Sussex words are derived will naturally have a special interest for many of my readers. All who collect or study strange words are anxious to know where they come from; and I confess that I was much surprised when I found that one of the first pieces of advice which was circulated among the members of the English Dialect Society was to abstain from etymology. It seemed to me that to encourage people to collect words, and at the same time to forbid them to attempt to give their derivations, was very like presenting a boy with a pair of skates and then desiring him on no account to go upon the ice. I little knew how treacherous was the element from which this humane society warns us off, till I was myself involved in its dangers, and only just rescued by the untiring efforts of the secretary, Mr. Skeat, from the consequences of rashness which might have been fatal to the success of my work.

Etymology is for many reasons surrounded with dangers and difficulties, not only on account of the prevalence and perpetuation of erroneous derivations already existing, on the authority of

15

persons who knew nothing whatever of the subject, but also because there are so few works published on the subject which are reliable.

Besides this, every amateur etymologist, who fancies he has made a fresh discovery, is led to make a series of wild shots at derivations, forgetting that it is the history of a word, and not the similarity of it to another in form or sound, which determines the source from which it is derived; so one mistake leads to others, and the confusion becomes every day worse confounded.

Still, I am aware that after all that can be said, word collectors will never be satisfied with merely collecting without deriving, and many of them will be at first inclined to resent any restriction of their liberties; therefore I hope that the English Dialect Society will take an early opportunity of buoying the dangerous channels of etymology, and give a few clear and distinct directions whereby we may be able to steer a safe course within certain defined limits.

The dialect of the Sussex people has been affected by the geographical position and the history of the county. It may be traced chiefly to Anglo-Saxon, Old Dutch, Old Welsh (or British), with a dash of 14th century French, and a little Scandinavian, the latter due to the sea-coast, which has for many generations invited hosts of friendly invaders to our shores, and has twice witnessed the landing of armies destined to influence the history and language of the whole country.

When the Roman legions landed on our coast they left an evidence of their appreciation of the Pevensey shrimps, which remains to this day in the word pandle, derived from the Latin pandulas, which is in constant use in this part of the county.

The arrival of the Normans, and the foundation of their large monastic establishments marks a very distinct phase in the history of our vocabulary.

But it will be observed that most of our words now in common use, denoting agricultural and domestic implements, are either to be traced to an Anglo-Saxon derivation, or actually retain their original Anglo-Saxon names in all purity of spelling and pronunciation. From this source also nearly all the Sussex surnames and names of villages and farms (following the dictionary) are derived. Nor must I forget to remark that when the Sussex peasant speaks of the sun as she, he uses an expression which clearly asserts his German origin.

As might be expected, many words are due to our proximity to the coast. The Sussex fishermen, in their constant intercourse with their Dutch and French brethren, although finding much difficulty in parleying to their satisfaction, have nevertheless for many generations adapted and introduced so many foreign words into common use among themselves, that their vocabulary is almost worthy of being called a fourth branch of the dialect.

Other circumstances, too, have tended to the increase of the French influence. Between 1562 and 1572 no less than 1,400 refugees from France settled themselves in Sussex, and many of their names may be still traced among our labouring people in the eastern division of the county. Besides this, the establishment of French prisoners in later times, and the custom which still prevails, though not so much as it did, of shopkeepers and townsfolk exchanging children with French families in order that each might learn enough of the other's language to be useful in after life, has kept the French element alive amongst us, and accounts for the existence of many words which are not so much derived from as positive corruptions of modern French.

Old House at Ditchling

But besides those words in the Sussex dialect which are really valuable as having been derived from authentic sources, there are a great many which are very puzzling to the etymologist, from the fact of their having been either actually invented without any reference to the laws of language, or adapted and corrupted from other words. A Sussex man has a great facility for inventing words. If he has any difficulty in expressing himself, he has no hesitation about forming a word for the occasion. This he does on the phonetic principle (if it can be said to be done on any principle at all), and as he prefers a long word, the result of his invention is generally very curious indeed; and whether or not the word serves the purpose for which it was intended, it is sure to be caught up by someone else, and, especially if it is a long one, is very soon incorporated among the words available for general use in the village.

There are also many words which are used to convey meanings totally different to their original intention. These may be called words of substitution. They are introduced in this way – a person hears a word which he does not quite understand; he does not take the trouble to ascertain either the meaning or pronunciation of it, but he uses a word something like it. This is specially the case with the names of complaints, such as will be found incidentally mentioned in some of the illustrations which I have given of the use of Sussex words, as, for instance, browncrisis for bronchitis, and rebellious for bilious, etc. The names of any but the most common trees and shrubs are also strangely perverted. A friend of mine had a gardener who persisted in calling an acacia the Circassian, and after much pains had been taken to point out the mistake, never got nearer than calling it the cash-tree. I have heard chrysanthemums called Christy anthems, and China asters Chaney oysters; but that was by the same man who also once enquired how I made out with "them Scotch-Chaney fowls" of mine.

It is also surprising how little trouble people will take to ascertain correctly even the names of their neighbours, and I know an instance of a man who lost sight of his own name altogether, from having been accustomed for many years to hear it mispronounced. But this in a great measure is to be attributed to the fact that a musical ear is very rarely found among Sussex people, a defect which is remarkably shown not only in the monotonous tunes to which their old songs are sung, but also in the songs themselves, which are almost entirely devoid of rhythm.

The Sussex pronunciation is, generally speaking, broad and rather drawling. It is difficult to say why certain long words are abbreviated, or why certain short words are expanded. In some names of places every syllable, and even every letter, is made the most of – as East Hoadlye for East Hoathly while others, like the name of my own village, are abruptly curtailed from three syllables to two by the most ruthless excision.

As far as I can reduce the pronunciation of the Sussex people to anything like a system it is this:–

a before double d becomes ar; whereby ladder and adder are pronounced larder and arder.

a before double l is pronounced like o; fallow and tallow become foller and toller.

a before t is expanded into ea; rate, mate, plate, gate, are pronounced réát, méát, péált, géát, they become almost dissyllables and probably perpetuate the true Anglo-Saxon vowel sounds.

a before ct becomes e; as satisfection for satisfaction.

e before ct becomes a; and affection, effect and neglect are pronounced affaction, effact and neglact.

Double e is pronounced as i in such words as sheep, week, called ship and wick; and the sound of double e follows the same rule in fild for field.

Having pronounced ee as i, the Sussex people in the most impartial manner pronounce i as ee, and thus mice, hive, dive become meece, heeve, and deeve.

i becomes e in pet for pit, spet for spit, and similar words.

io and oi change places respectively; and violet and violent become voilet and voilent, while boiled and spoiled are bioled and spioled.

o before n is expanded into oa in such words as pony, dont, bone; which are pronounced póány, dóánt and bóán. That is the long o of bone. The short o of ton and Monday tends to become a u as in ordinary English.

o before r is pronounced as a; as in carn and marning, for corn and morning.

o also becomes *a* in such words as rad, crass, and crap, for rod, cross, and crop.

ou is elongated into *aou* in words like hound, pound and mound; pronounced haound, paound and maound.

The final *ow*, as in many other counties, is pronounced *er*, as foller for fallow

The final *ow* after *r* becomes *r*, but is almost elided; as bar'r for barrow, vur'r for furrow.

The peculiarities with regard to the pronunciation of consonants are not so numerous as those of the vowels, but they are very decided and seem to admit of less variation.

Double *t* is always pronounced as *d*; as liddle for little, etc., and the *th* is invariably *d*; thus the becomes de; and these, them, theirs – dese, dem and deres. *d* in its turn is occasionally changed into *th*; as in fother for fodder.

The final *ps* in such words as wasp, clasp, and hasp are reversed to wapse, clapse and hapse. Or rather retain the Anglo-Saxon form.

Words ending in *st* have the addition of a syllable in the possessive case and the plural, and instead of saying "that some little birds had built their nests near the posts of Mr. Wests's gate," a Sussex boy would say "the birds had built their nestes near the postes of Mr. Westes' gate."

The Sussex half syllable is difficult to convey to one who has not heard it. The words bar'r and vur'r for barrow and furrow do not become actually monosyllabic, but the second syllable has no vowel sound and is barely distinguished from the first. Similarly the extended vowel as in geat for gate does not actually make the word a dissyllable, but very nearly does so.

f frequently becomes *v*, as in vur'r for furrow.

Thus I have tried as nearly as possible to define the rules of Sussex pronunciation – there are so many exceptions to all the rules that they can scarcely be called rules at all; but with regard to one letter a rule can be given which admits of no exception. The letter *h* is never by any chance used in its right place; and any one who has ever attempted to teach a Sussex child to read, must be convinced that nothing short of a surgical operation could ever introduce a correct pronunciation of the aspirate into his system.

This is unduly pessimistic. Many words are given in this dictionary both with and without the *h*. They are, in fact, usually very slightly aspirated. Over insistence on aspiration by teachers has such results as hood for wood.

I may here state that I have endeavoured to spell the words in this dictionary as nearly as possible as I have heard them pronounced; but in the examples of Sussex conversation, etc., I have not attempted to follow the exact pronunciation of the shorter words, because if I had done so, I should probably have rendered them incomprehensible to many of my readers and tiresome to all.

It now remains for me to state the principle upon which I have selected certain words for my dictionary, to the exclusion of others which have been given in the glossaries of Ray, Cooper, Halliwell and Holloway, as Sussex words.

I had to chose from,–

1. Words found only in some parts of Sussex;
2. Words found in Sussex only; and
3. Words found in Sussex, and also in other Counties.

With respect to the first two classes of words there was no question beyond that of identification, and as regards their identity as being actually in use in the county, I may say that I have by myself, or upon the authority of friends on whom I can rely, personally identified almost all of the eighteen hundred words which will be found in this collection. But the reader will easily understand that my chief difficulty has been in dealing with provincialisms unquestionably used in Sussex, but also in such common use elsewhere as apparently to deprive them of a distinctive character. The rule of my selection has been to include any provincial word not likely to have been adopted from a book, which I found in constant use among people who, as far as I could ascertain, had never been out of the county; and lest any of my readers should be inclined to complain of the admission of many words not distinctly belonging to Sussex, I have guarded myself in the title of the book I offer to their perusal, which is not only a dictionary of the Sussex dialect, but also a collection of provincialisms in use in

Petworth Churchyard

the County of Sussex.

I have also endeavoured to illustrate the use of the words by specimens of conversation, most of which are taken from the life verbatim, and will serve to indicate some phases of character and thought which find frequent expression among our people. When the opportunity has occurred I have added examples of folk lore and proverbial philosophy which are rapidly becoming obsolete, and if not recorded may in another generation be entirely forgotten. Many of them point to superstitions, which are remarkable from the very fact they should exist at all in the presence of our advanced civilization, and many more are connected with old customs already passed away.

I hope that they may at least serve the purpose of inducing some persons to look through the pages of my book, who would otherwise have taken no interest in a mere collection of words; and perhaps when they see how many interesting points may be elicited from closer intercourse with their poorer neighbours, they may be persuaded to become in their turn collectors of old words and stories of the past.

I am convinced that there are many more words yet to be recorded, and I hope that some of my readers will send me materials for a larger dictionary of the Sussex dialect, which I hope some day to be able to complete. I have little doubt of finding many persons ready to help me in this respect, for I have already received much assistance from persons who were strangers to me till they saw my name in connection with this publication; and even up to the last moment, while my work has been in the hands of the printers, several words have been sent to me too late to find a place in the alphabetical list. I have, therefore, requested the publishers to add at the end of each volume a few blank pages, so perforated as to be easily detached without injury to the book, in the hope that such persons as are willing to help me, may write down and forward to me any words not hitherto published which may come under their notice; adding always the name of the locality in which they are used, their pronunciation if it seems necessary, and any proverb or anecdote which may add to their interest.

In making this announcement I acknowledge the imperfection of my own work. Such a work must of necessity be tentative and imperfect, but such as it is I offer it to the kind perusal of all who are interested in the old-world ideas and language of our kind-hearted old-fashioned Sussex folk, many of whom I number among my dearest friends.

A Dictionary
OF THE
Sussex Dialect

Note: The letters, e, m, or w, after a word, indicates that it is used in East, Mid or West Sussex. By East is meant the extreme East of the County. The words marked with an asterisk are those which I have not myself been able to identify, but are given on the authority of the glossaries of Durrant Cooper, Halliwell, or Holloway.

Other abbreviations are:
Words from Kirkpatrick and Sharpe   †
Words from F. E. Sawyer, Brighton   §
Words from Jas. Fraser's book   ∞

A

A. The prefixed a-, as used in the Sussex dialect, generally adds some slight force or intensity, and is retained in such words as a-dry, a-lost, a-nigh, etc.

It is also almost invariably used with the participle; as, "I am a-going as soon as I can."

A-BEAR. [A-béran, Ang. Sax.] An old form of bear, in the sense of endure or like. Used in the negative, "I never could a-bear that chap."

A-BED. In bed.

ABIDE. [Abídan, Ang. Sax.] To endure. Used with the negative in the same way as a-bear. Can't abide 'em – don't like them.

ABILITY.† A word occurring in old account books for an assessment rate, now probably obsolete. As much as such an one ought, or is able, to pay.

ABOUTEN, e. [Abútan, Ang. Sax.] Just on the point of having done anything. Always used with a past tense; as, "I was abouten going out, when Master Noakes he happened along, and he kep' me." The syllable en is more frequently omitted in Sussex; as, "My knife wants sharping."

ABROAD, m. In all directions; all about.
"When e'er I take my walks abroad." I. Watts.

ABUSEFUL, m. Abusive.

ABUSEFULLY, m. In an abusive manner.
"As my missus was a-going home a Saddaday night, she met Master Chawbery a-coming out of the Red Lion, and he treated her most

The Land Gate, Rye

abusefully, and threw abroad all her shop-goods. He's a man as aint no account at all aint Master Chawbery."

ACCOUNT. Esteem; reputation. "The Princes both make high account of you." – Richard III., Act iii. sc. 2.

ACHE, e. To tire "I am afraid you'll ache waiting so long."
To long for anything. "Nancy just will be pleased, she has ached after a dole I don't know the time when."

ADIN. [Corruption of Within.] The initial w is mostly omitted in Sussex; and th is always pronounced as d; thus, the wood becomes de 'ood; and within idin or adin.

ADLE. [Ang. Sax., ádl.] Pronounced ardle. Stupid. "He's an adle-headed fellow."

ADONE. [Have done.] Leave off. I am told on good authority that when a Sussex damsel says "Oh! do adone," she means you to go on; but when she says "Adone-do," you must leave off immediately.

ADRY. Thirsty.

AFEARD. [Afæred, Ang. Sax.] Afraid.
"Hal, art thou not horribly afeared?" – I Henry IV., Act ii. sc. 4.

AGARVES, m. May berries. Haws.

Also called Aigarces, Argarces Argaves, Eggas or Eggas-berries, (q.v.) Hogarves, (q.v.) Hogasses, Hog-gazels, (q.v.) and Hoghazels.

AGIN. [Agen, Ang. Sax.] Near to; against.

"He lived up agin the Church, and died about forty yeere agoo."

AGOO. Ago.

AGREEABLE. Acquiescent; consenting.

"They asked me if I'd come in and have a cup o' tea, and I was quite agreeable;" meaning that he accepted the invitation.

AGWAN. Going.

ALL-ON, m. Incessantly.

"He kept all-on making a noise."

ALL-ONE. All the same; as,

"Well, 'tis all-one whether ye do or whether ye döant."

ALLOW. To give as an opinion. To conclude.

"As I was agwaine down the street, I ses to Master Nappet ses I, what d'ye think of this here job down at the blacksmith's? I ses, and Master Nappet he allowed that it was amost too bad!"

"I allowed you was over twenty" = thought you were.

"I allus allowed she were 'ees darter."

ALLTSINIT, m. [All that's in it.] Merely.

ALONG-OF. On account of. "Along of her it was that we met here so strangely" – Cymbeline, Act v. sc. 5.

This expression is often expanded into allalong-of, and even, all-through along-on-account-of; as "Master Piper he lost his life all-through-along-on account-of drink."

AMENDMENT, m. Manure. Also called Manner.

"You go down to the ten-acre field, and spread that amendment abroad, and peck up them ammut-castes."

AMMUT-CASTÈS. Emmet-castes; ant-hills. (Worm-casts.)

This form of plural is invariably retained in words ending with st, as postes, nestes. The reduplicated plural is also not unfrequently used; and a Sussex man would see nothing absurd in saying, –
"I saw the ghostesses
Sitting on the postesses
Eating of their toastesses
And fighting with their fistesses."

AMMUTS, m. Emmets; ants.

AMOST. Almost.

AMPER.* A flaw or fault in linen or woollen cloth. A tumour or swelling.

AMPERY, m. [Ampre, Ang. Sax., a flaw.] Beginning to decay, especially applied to cheese.

AMPERY. Weak; unhealthy.

AMPRE-ANG.* A decayed tooth.

AN. Of. "If you wants to be rid an him, you lend him a sixpence; I lay he'll never come anigh you no more."

ANCLEY, m., ANCLIFF, c. Ankle. Also Ankley.

ANCLIFF-BONE. In East Sussex, I have put out my ancliff-bone, is equivalent to I have sprained my ankle.

ANDIRONS. (Possibly from Brand irons). Fire dogs.

The ornamental irons on each side of the hearth in old fire-places, before grates were introduced. The andirons were sometimes made of superior metal, or gilt, and of very large dimensions. "Her andirons (I had forgot them) were two winking cupids of silver." – Cymbeline, Act ii. sc. 4.

The derivation of this word is obscure, see Brands, or Brandirons.

ANEWST.* [Neawest, Ang. Sax.] Nigh; almost; near at hand.

ANIGH. Nigh; near.

ANYWHEN. At any time. This word is very usual in Sussex.

APPLETERRE.* [Apple and terre, French.] An orchard.

APPLETY e. [Apple and tye, an enclosure.] An apple-loft, where the fruit is kept. This word is used on the borders of Kent, in which county the word tye means an enclosure, whereas in Sussex it means an open common.

APSE. [Æpse, Ang. Sax.] An aspentree.

ARDER. An adder. In Sussex the letters a and e are often pronounced as in French.

The country people say that an adder can never die till sunset. If it be cut to pieces, the bits will retain their vitality till the sun goes down. They also say that on the adder's belly will be found the words, –

"If could hear as well as see,
No man in life could masta me."

"Them there deadly arders" is the usual phrase.

ARG, m. To argue; to wrangle. "These chapelfolks always wants to arg."

ARGIFY, m. To signify; to import. "I do'ant know as it argifies much whether I goos to-day or whether I goos to-morrow.'

Also argue, "Don't argify with me Miss."

ARTER. [Corruption of After.]

ASH-CLOTH, m.† Before the use of soda was understood, the washer women used to soften the

Ditchling

27

Coombes Church

water by straining it through a coarse cloth, which was fastened over the top of the wash tub and first covered with marshmallow leaves, and then with a layer of wood ashes.

ASHEN. Made of the wood of the ash.

ASLEW, m. Aslant.

ATWEEN. Between. Also used in the Eastern Counties.

ATWIXT. Betwixt.

AUMRY, e. [Aumoire, Old French, a cupboard.] or

AWMRY, e. A large chest.
  "And when they had eaten, King Arthur made great clerks to come before him that they should chronicle the high adventures of the good knights; and all was made great books and put in almeries at Salisbury." – Sir Thomas Malory's Morte D'Arthur.

AVISED, e. [Aviser, French]. Aware of. To know for a certainty.
  "I'm well avised that John spent all his wages at the Barley-mow."

AWHILE. For a time.
  "We shan't have no gurt frostes yet awhile – not atwixt now and Christmas, very like."

AXEY, e. The ague. A complaint which is very prevalent in many parts of Sussex. There is a different name for it in almost every district. In some places it is believed that it may be cured by the following charm, which, to be efficacious, must be written on a three-cornered piece of paper and worn round the neck till it drops off, –
  "Ague, ague, I thee defy,
      Three days shiver,
      Three days shake,
  Make me well for Jesus' sake!"
Some other names are Johnny, Old Johnny and Lord John.

B

BACKSTAYS, or BACKSTERS. Wide flat pieces of board, made like snow shoes, which are strapped on the feet and used by the fishermen in walking over the loose beach or soft mud on the seashore.

BACKTURNED, m, and **BACKWENT, m.** These words, which are evidently of Saxon construction, can only be explained by giving instances of their use. "He was backturned when I saw him," means "he was standing with his back to me." "I only saw him backwent," means "I only saw him as he was going away from me."

BAIL, w. † The handle of a bucket, pail or kettle. That is the loop handle.

BAIT, m. Afternoon refreshment, with which strong beer is given, in the hay and harvestfield.

BALDERDASH.* [Probably derived from Ang. Sax. Baldwyrda, a saucy jester.] Obscene conversation. More usually nonsense.

BALLET m. A ballad.

BANNICK, m. To beat.
"I'll give him a good bannicking if I catch him."

BART. To cough.
"I can't abear for my master to goo to church; for he keeps up such a barking, that nobody can't hear naun for him."

BARLEY-CHAMPER, w., BARLEY-HUMMELER, BARLEY NIBBLER, or **BARLEY-NOLLER.**
A barley-awner. An instrument for cutting off the beards of the barley.

BARWAY, m. & e. A field-gate, made of bars or rails so fitted as to draw out from the posts.

BAT. [Bâton, French, a stick.] Or much more likely from bat, Ang. Sax., a bat, club, staff. A rough walking-stick.

BATCH. A quantity of bread baked at once without heating the oven afresh.
"How now, thou core of envy?
Thou crusty batch of nature
what's the news?" – Troilus and Cressida, Act v. sc. 1.

BATFOWLER. One who takes birds at night with a large folding-net on long poles, called a bat-fowling net.
Gon: "You are gentlemen of brave metal; you would lift the moon out of her sphere, if she would continue in it five weeks without changing."
Steb: "We would so, and then go a bat-fowling." – Tempest, Act ii. sc. 1.

BATS.† Logs of wood for burning, or any odd pieces of wood.

BATTER. [Abattre, French, to beat down.] A wall which diminishes upwards is said to batter.

BAVINS. Pronounced Bah'vn. Brushwood faggots.
"The skipping king, he ambled up and down,
With shallow justers and rash bavin wits,
Soon kindled, and soon burnt."
– I Henry IV, Act iii. sc. 2.

BAWL, e. To read aloud.
A mother said of a child who did not go to school on account of illness, "I keeps him to his book all the same, and his father likes to hear him bawl a bit in the evening."

BAY. A pond-head (or dam) made up to a sufficient height to keep in store water.

BAY. A compartment of a barn. the space between the main beams of the roof: so that a barn crossed twice with beams is a barn of three bays.
"If this law hold in Vienna ten years, I'll rent the fairest house in it, after three-pence a bay." – Measure for Measure, Act iii. sc. 2.

BE. A common prefix to verbs, generally conveying a reflective and intensive power, as be-smeared, be-muddled, be-spangled.

BEACH, m. Shingle brought from the sea-coast is always called beach, as opposed to the inland gravel.

BEAT THE DEVIL ROUND THE GOOSEBERRY-BUSH, e. To tell a long rigmarole story without much point.
An old man at Rye said he did not think the new curate was much of a hand in the pulpit, he did beat the devil round the gooseberry-bush so.

BEAZLED, m. Completely tired out.
"He comes home tired of an evening, but not beazled like boys who go to plough."
"I be fair beazled."

BECK. [Becc, Ang. Sax., a brook.] A rivulet.

BECK, w. [Becca, Ang. Sax., a pick-axe.] A mattock.

TO BECK, is to use the beck or mattock.

BEEPOT. A beehive.

BEESKEP, e. [Scep, Ang. Sax, a basket.] A beehive, or the straw hackle placed over the hive to protect it.
There is a superstition in the county, that if a piece of black crape is not put round the hive after a death in the family, the bees will die.

BEEVER, w.
Eleven o'clock luncheon

BEEVES, m. A corruption of Bee hives; the i in the word hives being pronounced as in French.
"Well, John, how are you going to make out this winter?"
"Well, I reckon I shall have to make brooms and beeves."

BEGRIDGE, m. To grudge.

BEHITHER, e. On this side. It answers to beyond.
"The fifty-first milestone stands behither the village, and the fifty-second beyond."

BEING. An abode; a lodging.
"Return he cannot, nor
Continue where he is,
to shift his being,
Is to exchange one misery for another."
– Cymbeline, Act i. sc. 6.

BELEFT, m. Perfect of believe.
"I never should have beleft that he'd have gone on belvering and swearing about it as he did."

BELVER, m. To make an angry disturbance.

BENCH. A widow's bench is the share of the husband's estate which a woman enjoys besides her jointure.

BEST, m. To get the better of anyone; to beat at any game.
"I bested him every time."

BETHERED, e. Bed-ridden.

Glynde

"Poor creature! She was bethered three years before she died."

BETHWINE. The wild clematis. C. vitalba. Tom-bacca. Also called Pethwine.

BETTERMOST. Superior; above average. Generally qualified by the word rather.

"The new people whe have come to live down at the cottage seem rather bettermost sort of folks."

BIBLER-CATCH, w. [Bilboquet, French.] The game of cup and ball.

BIDE. [Bidan, Ang. Sax., to remain.] To wait; remain; stay.
"If ye've got one you can run;
If ye've got two you may goo;
But if ye've got three
You must bide where you be."
Sussex Proverbial Advice to a Young Mother.

BILLUS, w. To beat; to flog.

BIND-DAYS, w. Days on which the tenants of certain manors were bound to work for their lord.

31

BINE, m. The hop stalk which binds round the pole.

BISCUIT. In Sussex the words biscuit and cake interchange their usual meaning. A plum biscuit, or a seed biscuit, means a plain cake made of either of these ingredients.

BISHOP-BARNABY, e. The lady-bird. In some parts of Sussex the lady-bird is` called the lady-bug; (lady-cow); in others, fly-golding, or God Almighty's cow, by which singular name it is also known in Spanish (Vaca de Dios). The children set the insect on their finger and sing, –

"Bishop Bishop-Barnabee,
Tell me when my wedding shall be
If it be to-morrow day
Open your wings and fly away."

BITTEN, m. [Bitende, Ang. Sax., biting.] Inclined to bite.
"Mind that dog, he's terrible bitten."

BITTLE, w. A wooden milk bowl.

BITTLE-BATTLE. The game of stoolball.

There is a tradition that this game was originally played by the milk maids with their milking-stools, which they used for bats; but this word makes it more probable that the stool was the wicket, and that it was defended with the bittle, which would be called the bittle-bat; hence the word bittle-battle.

BLACKEYED SUSAN, m., or POND PUDDING. A well pudding, with plums or raisins in it.

BLACK-GRASS, e.† Alopecurus agrestis. Fox-tail grass.

BLAME. A common substitute for a worse word.
"Blame ye! ye be always at

something; be blamed if I döant give it yer one of these days."

BLANKET-PUDDING, m. A long, round pudding, made of flour and jam; sometimes called a bolster-pudding.

BLEAT, m. Cold; cutting; applied to the wind.

BLOBTIT; m. [Blabbe, Mid. Eng., to blab.] A tell-tale.

BLOBTONGUE, w.† [Blabbre, Danish, to gabble.] A tell-tale. (See Blobtit.)

BLUE-BOTTLE, m.† The wild hyacinth.

BLUNDER, m. A noise as of something heavy falling.
"I heard a terrible blunder over head."

BLUNDER. To make a noise.

BLUV, or BLIV. [Corruption of Believe.] "I bluv" is often used at the end of an assertion in the sense of "you may take my word for it," as "'Taint agoing to rain to-day, I bluv."

BLY, e. [Bleo, Ang. Sax., hue.] A resemblance; a general likeness.
"I can see a bly of your father about you."

BOBBINGNEEDLE, m. A bodkin.

BOCO, e. [Beaucoup, French, much.] A large quantity.
This word is principally used by the fishermen.

BODGE, w.† A water cask on wheels.

BODGER. Corruption of badger.

BOFFLE. A confusion or mistake.
"If you sends him of a errand he's purty sure to make a boffle of it."

BOKE. [Bealcian, Ang. Sax.] To nauseate.

BOND.† [Bond, Ang. Sax.] A band, as a hay-bond, bonds for fastening up the sheaves of corn. etc.

BONDLAND, w. (Bonda, Ang. Sax.; Bondi, Icelandic, a cultivator.) Cultivated land. Used in Framfield and Mayfield for old cultivated or yard-lands, as distinguished from assart-lands, which were parts of forests cleared of wood and put into a state of cultivation, for which rents were paid under the name of assart-rents.

BOOK. The Bible is almost always spoken of by old people as the Book. Not many years ago the family Bible was the only book to be found in the cottages of the poor; now the frequent visits of the book-hawker have introduced a taste for reading into the remotest districts of the county, but still the Bible retains its title of the Book; and I was glad to hear a rough-looking carter boy say the other day, "I always read a bit of my Book before I goos to bed."

BOOK.† A word used in old parochial accounts for a rate, as "a 2s. 6d. book produces £500 in Horsted Keynes."

BOOT-LEGS, m. Short gaiters, not reaching to the knee.

BOSTAL or BORSTAL. A pathway up a hill, generally a very steep one, and on the northern escarpment of the Downs; as the White Bostal near Alciston, the Ditchling Bostal, etc.

With respect to the derivation of this much-disputed word, Professor Bosworth has kindly given me the following: – Burg-stal, -stol, es; m. [burg, beorg, beorh, a hill, stal a place, seat, dwelling]. A hill-seat, dwelling on a hill; sedes super collem vel clivum, Cot. 209. The names of places built on a hill, as Burstall- in Suffolk, Borstall in Kent and Oxfordshire, etc.

Mr. Kemble (Sussex Archeological Collection, vol. II, p. 292) takes "the first word of the compound to be the Saxon word beorh, a hill or mountain, the passing of which into bor, is neither unusual nor surprising. The second word is not so easily determined. Were the word ever written borstill, Mr. K should suggest the Saxon stigel, a stile or rising path; and beorh-stigel would be the hill-path or mountain path. He does not know whether, in that branch of the West Saxon which prevailed in Sussex, 'steal' did signify a road or way; but it is not without probability that some of the Anglo-Saxon dialects might have justified that use of the term; for 'stealian' or 'stellan' does sometimes seem to be applied in the sense of 'going or leaping'."

BOTTOM, m. A valley in the Downs. Also in the Weald any flat land near water.

BOTTOM. A reel of cotton.

BOUGE, m. [Bouge, French.] A water cask. The round swelling part of a cask.

BOUGH-HOUSE, m. A private house allowed to be open at fairs for the sale of liquor.

An old person describing the glories of Selmeston fair, which has now been discontinued many years, said "There was all manner of booths and bough houses." In former times putting up boughs upon anything was an indication that it was to be sold, and a bush at the end of a pole was the badge of a country ale house; which gave rise to the proverb, "Good wine needs no bush," i.e., nothing to point out where it is sold.

BOULDER-HEAD. A work against the sea, made up of small wooden stakes.

BOUT. A day's work.

"I shan't do it this bout," means, I shall not finish to-day.

BOZZLER, m. A parish constable; a sheriff's officer.

BRABAGIOUS, e. An adjective of reproach, the exact meaning of which is difficult to determine; but it is generally considered available for use in a quarrelsome discussion between females. "You nasty brabagious creature." It seems to combine the advantages of Mrs. Gamp's two principal epithets, bragian and bage.

BRAKE. The common fern. Pteris aquilina. Plural, bracken.

"I'll run from thee and hide me in the brakes." – Mid. Night's Dream, Act ii. sc. 2.

BRAKE. A kneading trough.

BRANDS, BRAND DOGS, or BRANDIRONS. Irons used for supporting the brands for burning wood in a wood fire.

BRAVE, m. [Brave, French.] Well in health.

"How are you, John?"
"I'm bravely, thank you."

BRA VE, m. Prosperous.

"I have been making out bravely since you were last here."

BREACHY. Brackish, applied to water.

BREACHY. [Brèche, French, a breach.] A word applied to cattle which are wild and liable to break through the fences.

BREAD-AND-BUTTERS, m. [Compare, Butter-brod, German.] Pronounced brenbutters; Slices of bread buttered; used in the same way as the French word tartine.

Cowdray

BREAD-AND-CHEESE-FRIEND, e. A true friend as distinguished from a cupboard-lover.

"He's a regular brencheese friend he is, not like a good many, always after what they can get."

BREAK.† A cultivator used among potatoes and hops.

BRICKS; m. The paved walk in front of a cottage, or paved path in a garden.

"I'm always pleased to see him a'coming up my bricks."

BRITT, m. [Brytan, Ang. Sax., to break]. To shatter like hops from being over-ripe.

BROACH, w. [Broche, French.] A spit.
"Broached with the steely point of Clifford's lance." –
III Henry VI, Act ii. sc. 3.

BROKE, w.† A large quantity of timber.

BRONK, m. A disdainful toss of the head

"She didn't choose to see me, so she just gave a bronk and passed on."

BROOK, m. A water meadow.

BROOM-CLISHER, m. [Clish, a bond.] A broom maker.

BROOM-DASHER, m. BROOM

SQUIRE, w. A dealer in faggots, brooms, etc. The word dasher is also combined in haberdasher.

BROWN-BIRD, m. Thrush. Also called Grey bird; but grey-bird is really the missel-thrush.

BRUFF, e. Rough; short in manners and speech.

BRUSS, m. [Compare French Brusque, blunt.] Proud; upstart. One who spoke bluntly and briskly was "bruss".

" 'E were crass too, 'e spoke monstrus bruss to me."

BRUSTLES. [Variations of Bristles.]

BRUTTE, e. [Brouter, French, to nibble.] To browse or feed upon.

BRUTTLE. Always in Sussex used for brittle.

BUCKING, m. [Buc, Ang. Sax., a tub.] A washing of clothes.

BUD, w. A calf of the first year, so called because the horns then begin to appear or bud.

BUDDY, w. Stupid, in the same sense as the word calf is often used for a stupid fellow.

BUDGE, w. [Bouge, French.] A cask placed on wheels for carrying water.

Malthouse Farm, Hurstpierpoint

BUDGE, m. [Bouder, French, to pout.] Grave; solemn.

"He looked very budge when I asked him who stole the apples."

BUG. Any hard-winged insect.

BULLOCK, m. A fat beast of either sex.

I was very much astonished when I first heard a farmer say, "Yes, she's a purty cow, a very purty cow indeed, and one of these days she'll make a nice bullock."

BULLOCK-LEAZE.† The right of turning one bullock out on a common to graze. (Used at Berwick and other places.)

BUMBLESOME, m. Hunched up; misfitting. Also, ineffectively fussy.

BUMBOO, m. A mysterious compound of spirituous liquors, under the influence of which, Mr. Turner, draper, of Easthoathly, made the following entry in his diary:– "1756 (Sunday), April 28th. I went down to Jones', where we drank one bowl of punch and two muggs of bumboo, and I came home again in liquor. Oh! with what horrors does it fill my heart to think I should be guilty of doing so, and on a Sunday too! Let me once more endeavour, never, no never, to be guilty of the same again."

BUNCH, m. A swelling.

"It came out in bunches all over me."

BUNGER, m. (Pronounced 'bunjer.')

To do anything awkwardly.

BUNNY, w. A wooden or brick drain laid under a road or gateway to carry off the water; also called a cocker.

BUNT, e. To rock a cradle with the foot; to push or butt. A bunt is described to me as a push with a knock in it, or a knock with a push in it.

"I'll give you a middlin' bunt prensley if you döant keep still."

BUNTER, m. An old-fashioned machine for cleaning corn.

BURGH, m. [Burg, Ang. Sex.] A rising ground; a hillock. The term is frequently applied to the barrows or tumuli on the Downs.

BURNISH, e. To grow fat. The expression, "You burnish nicely," meaning, "You look well," is frequently used in East Sussex, and is meant as a compliment.

BURY.† (Pronounced ' berry.') A rabbit hole; a hole made by any animal.

BUTTER-MY-WIG, m. A strong asseveration. (sic).

"No I wunt; butter my wig if I will!"

BYSTE, m. A couch made up of two chairs for a child to sleep upon in the day-time.

BYSTE, m. To lie down in the day time.

"I was quite took to (ashamed) to think you should have come in the other day and found me bysted, but I was quite entirely eat up with the rheumatics, and couldn't get about no hows."

BY-THE-BYE, e. By chance.

"He come along one day by-the-bye, or else he hasn't been a-nigh me for the last ten years."

BYTHEN. By the time that.

"Bythen you've come back 'twill be coager-time."

C

CAB.* [Cabaler, French, to plot.] A small number of persons secretly united in the performance of some undertaking.

CADGER. Not only a travelling beggar, but anyone given to begging is called by this name in Sussex

CAFFINCHER, w.† The Chaffinch.

CALL OUT OF NAME, m. To call a person out of his name is not to give him his proper title. Or to revile him.

"And then, what d'ye think he says? Why, he says ' 'ooman' and I aint a-going to be called out of my name by such a fellow as him, I can promise him."

CALL-OVER, m. To abuse.

"He come along here a cadging, and fancy he just did call me over, because I told him as I hadn't got naun to give him."

CALLOW, m. [Calo, Ang. Sax., bald.] Smooth; bare. The woods are said to be getting callow when they are just beginning to bud out. Also said of young chicks.

CAMBER, e. A harbour.

Winchelsea Castle, built to protect Rye Harbour, is called Camber

CAMSTEERY, e. A horse is said to be very camsteery when it does not go steadily. In Northumberland the word means crazy

CANT. To upset or let fall.

"The cart canted over and he was canted out into the road."

CANT. A corner of a field.

A haystack is said to be cut across in cants, and a field of wheat is divided into cants when it is partitioned out in slips for the reapers, each of whom takes one or more cants as his share of work.

CARDIOUS †. A mixed cloth made of wool and linen thread. A word which frequently occurred in old account books when spinning-wheels were in use.

CARFAX. [Carrefourgs, Old French, crossways.] A Partways; A place where four (or more) roads meet, but do not form a cross, as the Carfax at Horsham.

CARP-PIE*. To eat carp-pie is to submit to another person's carping at your actions.

CARRIERS.† Part of a spinning wheel fitted with wire hooks through which the thread passed to the reel.

CAST.† The second swarm from a hive.

CATCH HOT, e. To take fever.

CATCH HURT, m. To meet with an accident. An old man once told me that he catched hurt at Chiddingly Church, meaning that he got married there.

CATERCROSS, w. Slanting.

CATERING, m. From corner to corner.

CATERWISE, m. Diagonally.

"If you goos caterwise across the field you'll find the stile."

CATS TAILS. The male blossom of hazel or willow.

CATTERNING. To go catterning is to go round begging for apples and beer for a festival on St. Catherine's Day, and singing, –

"Cattern' and Clemen' be here, here, here,

Ashdown Forest from East Grinstead

Give us your apples and give us your
     beer,
One for Peter,
Two for Paul,
Three for him who made us all
Clemen' was a good man,
Cattern' was his mother;
Give us your best,
And not your worst
And God will give your soul good
     rest."

CAULKER-BRIDGE, w.† A rough
bridge made of logs and fagots.

CAVINGS, w. [Ceaf, Ang. Sax.,
chaff.] The short straws or ears
which are raked off the corn when
it is thrashed.

CERTAIN SURE, e.
     The superlative of certainly.

"I hope you are pretty well
to-day, certain sure indeed!"

CHACKET, m. To cough.

CHAMP, w. Firm; hard.
     "The river has a champ bottom."

CHANCE-BORN, c.
     An illegitimate child. Or a
Come-by-chance or love-child.

CHANGES. Shirts and shifts.
     If you ask what a girl or boy
stands most in need of on first
going to service, you are sure to be
told "changes." "I have not got a
change means, I have no linen."
The following inventory of the
outfit of a girl going to service is
taken from the account book of
Selmeston parish, 1745: –

"An account of Grace Barber's cloaths, – 14 caps and moobs, 2 changes, one gown, 2 white hancerchifs, 3 coats, 2 spackol hancerchifs, one white apron, 2 other aprons."

CHAPEL-MASTER, m.
A dissenting preacher.

CHARGER, e. A large platter or meat dish.
"And his head was brought in a charger." – St. Matthew. xiv. 11.

CHARM-STUFF, e.
Ague medicine.
In Sussex, medicine is generally spoken of as physical medicine, but it is carefully distinguished from doctor's stuff, by which a tonic is meant.
The use of charms, especially in cases of ague or wounds, is still prevalent in the country; and the following charm is not unfrequently used for the cure of a burn. It must be repeated three times, –
"Two Angels from the North,
One brought fire, one brought frost:
Out fire, in frost,
In the name of the Father, the Son, and the Holy Ghost."

CHASTISE, m. To accuse. To upbraid.
"They've been chastising my boy of setting the fagot-stack a-fire."

CHAVISH, e., and w. A chattering or prattling noise of many persons speaking together.
A noise made by a flock of birds.

CHECK, m. To reproach or taunt.
"He checked him of his cousin Tom (who had been sent to prison)."

CHEE, e. A hen-roost. Going to chee is going to roost.

CHEQUER, w. The service tree. Pyrus torminalis. The fruit is called chequers, serbs, or sorbs.

CHESS, e. A plaid.
"I bought a chess shawl for mother."

CHICK. In East Sussex used as the plural of chicken.
"I reckon you have got a good sight of chick here."

CHICKEN. In Mid Sussex used as the plural of chick.

CHILL. To take off the extreme coldness from any beverage by placing it before the fire.
"I often gets my mistus to chill a drop of beer for me, when I comes home winter evenings."

CHIP, w.† The wooden part of a plough to which the share is fastened.

CHIPPER, w.† Lively: cheerful.

CHIZZLE. w. Bran.

CHIZZLY, e. [Ceosel, Ang. Sax., sand.] Gritty; harsh and dry under the teeth.

CHOCK. To choke, Dry.

CHOCKLY, m. Chokey, dry.

CHOGS, m. The refuse cuttings of the hop plants when dressed in the spring before being polled.

CHOICE, m. Careful.
"He ain't got but two brockyloes, but he's middlin' choice over them I can tell ye."

CHOPPER, w. A fried pig's face. I.e. chap.

CHOW, e. To chew.
"The old cow's better this morning, she's up and chowing her quid."

CHUCKER, m. Cosily; to chucker oneself is to chuckle over anything.

"They chatted along quite friendly and chucker."

CHUCKLE- HEADED. Stupid.

CHUCKS, m. Large chips of wood.

CHUFF, m. Churlish; surly.

"The old gentleman he went out to get a few chucks, and there they was, a sitting in the wood-house together jes' as chucker; and he was middlin' chuff about it, I bluv!"

CHURCH-BAWLED, or CHURCH-CRIED, m. Having the banns published in church.

The tradition in Sussex is that if a person goes to church to hear himself cried, his children will be born deaf and dumb.

CHURCH-LITTEN, m. [Licthn, Ang. Sax., a burying-place.] A church-yard.

CHURCH-STEEPLE, w.† The common agrimony. Agrimonia rupatoria.

CLAM. [Clam, Ang. Sax., anything that holds or retains.] A rat-trap.

CLAPPER. The tongue.
"He hath a heart as sound as a bell, and his tongue is the clapper, for what his heart thinks his tongue speaks." – Much Ado About Nothing. Act iii. sc. 2.

CLAVELS, w. The separate corns in an ear of wheat.

CLEAT, e. A piece of wood placed to prevent a door or gate from swinging backwards and forwards.

CLEAT-BOARDS, w. Mud pattens; broad flat pieces of board fastened on the shoes to enable a person to walk on the mud without sinking into it; much used by the eel-spearers at Chichester harbour and elsewhere.

CLEMMENING. Going round from house to house asking for apples and beer for St. Clement's Day.

In spite of a proclamation made at London, July 22, 1540, that "neither children should be decked ne go about upon St. Nicholas,' St. Catherine, St. Clement, the Holy Innocents' and such-like days," the children in some parts of East Sussex still keep up the custom of catterning and clemmening, and the Sussex black-smiths are particularly active in commemorating their patron saint; the anvils are fired with a loud explosion, and at least a half-holiday is kept. At Burwash, a few years ago, it was the custom to dress up a figure with a wig and beard and a pipe in his mouth, and set it up over the door of the inn where the blacksmiths feasted on St. Clement's day. Nov. 23.

CLIM. To climb.

CLINKERS. Small bricks burnt very hard and used for paving. The hard refuse cinders from a forge fire.

CLISH, m. The bond or band by which heath or birch brooms are fastened.

CLOCKSMITH, m. A watchmaker.

"I be quite lost about time, I be; for I've been forced to send my watch in to the clocksmith. I couldn't make no sense of mending it myself; for I'd iled it and I'd biled it, and then I couldn't do more with it."

CLOGUE, m. To flatter.

CLOPPERS, or CLOG-BOOTS.

Boots with wooden soles, worn by the fishermen on some parts of the coast.

CLOSE, w. A farmyard. Walled or any walled inclosure.

CLOVERLAY. [Clæfer and leag, Ang. Sax.] A field of clover which has been lately mown.

CLUCK, m. Out of spirits; slightly unwell. A hen is said to be cluck when she wants to sit.

CLUNG, m. Cold and damp.

The mown grass is spoken of as very clung after having been exposed to wet chilly weather, so that it has not hayed satisfactorily.

CLUTCH, e. Close; tightly.

"If you takes up a handful of the hay and holds it pretty clutch, you'll soon see 'taint fit to carry, for 'tis terr'ble clung."

CLUTTER, w. A brood of chickens or a covey of partridges.

CLUTTER-UP, m. To throw into confusion.

COAGER, m. Luncheon. Pronounced 'cojer'. Called in some parts of the county an elevener, (usually said 'levener',) from the time at which it is generally taken by the labourers.

COAGER-CAKE. A plain cake is

Hogh Street, Southover

often baked as the couger cake, for the week's consumption.

COARSE, e. Rough; stormy; applied to weather.

COARSE, e. Childish.

"She is twelve years old, but she is so coarse for her years that you would not take her to be but ten."

COAST.* [Coste, Old French, a rib.] The ribs of cooked meat, particularly lamb.

COBBLE-STONES. Pebbles on the seashore.

COCKER, w. A culvert; a drain under a road or gate.

COCKER-UP. To spoil; to gloss over with an air of truth.

"You see this here chap of hers he's cockered-up some story about having to goo away somewheres up into the sheeres; and I tell her she's no call to be so cluck over it; and for my part I dunno but what I be very glad an't, for he was a chap as was always a cokeing about the cupboards, and cogging her out of a Sunday."

COCKS.§ [Kog. Kogge. Danish.] Small boats, from two to six tons burden, used in the herring fishery. Their period of fishing was called cock-fare, and their nets cock-heaks.

CODDLE, e. or COCKLE, w. To parboil.

Apples so cooked are called coddled apples.

CODGER. A miser a stingy old fellow.

COG, m. [Cogger, Old English, a trickster.] To entice.

"I cannot flatter, and speak fair, Smile in men's faces, smooth, deceive, and cog." – Richard III, Act i. sc. 3.

COILERS. (See Quilers.)

COKE, m. [Kijken, Dutch, to peep about. To pry about.

COMB, m. An instrument used by thatchers. Also called a Rake comb, it is used to comb out the straw when being laid on, for trimming up ricks and stacks and to measure up the work.

COME. When such a time arrives.

"I shall be eighty-two come Lady-tide."

COMMENCE, m. An affair; a job.

"Here's a pretty commence."

COMP, m. [Comp, Ang. Sax.] A valley.

Some cottages in the parish of Beddington are called by this name, from which also the name of the village of Compton is derived.

CONCERNED IN LIQUOR, e. Drunk. This is one of the many expressions used in Sussex to avoid the word drunk. To have had a little beer, means to have had a great deal too much; to have half-a-pint otherwhile, means to be an habitual drunkard; to be none the better for what he had took, means to be much the worse; to be noways tossicated, implies abject helplessness.

A Sussex man may be tight, or concerned in liquor, but drunk never!

In the village of Selmeston the blacksmith's shop is next door to the public-house. I have met numbers of people going up to the forge, but never one going to the Barley-mow.

CONEY, m. A rabbit.

"There is no remedy: I must coney-catch, I must shift."—Merry Wives of

Windsor, Act i. sc. 3.

CONTRAIRY. [Contraire, French.] Disagreeable; obstinately self-willed.

A man describing his deceased wife, to whom he was really very much attached, said, "She was a very nice, pleasant 'ooman as long as no one didn't interrupt her, but if you had ever so few words with her, she'd be just as contrairy as ever was a hog."

CONTRAPTION, m. Contrivance; management.

A pedlar's pack is spoken of sometimes as his contraption.

COOCH-GRASS. [Cwic, Ang. Sax.]

A course, bad species of grass, which grows very rapidly on arable land, and does much mischief by the long stringy roots which it throws out in great quantities.

Barnes says, with reference to this – Cooch, couch grass, quitch grass, creeping wheat grass, Triticum repens. Mr. Vernon suggests that it was originally quick grass, from its lively growth. More likely creeping grass because it grows creeping low under the ground. (in heraldry, couchant, lying.)

COOLTHE, e. Coolness.

"I set the window open for coolthe."

COOMBE, or COMBE, m. [Cwm, Welsh, a valley.] A hollow in the Downs; especially one in an escarpment.

This word is to be traced in the names of many Southdown villages and farms, such as Telscombe, Ashcombe, etc.

COP, e. To throw; to heap anything up. Especially with regard to corn.

COPSON, w. A fence placed on the top of a small dam laid across a ditch for the purpose of keeping sheep from going over it.

CORD. A cord of wood is a pile of wood cut up for burning, 8 ft. by 4 ft. and 4 ft. thick.

CORDBATS, or CORD WOOD, m. Large pieces of wood, roots, etc., set up in stacks. Cut to the cord length of 4 ft. or 3 ft.

CORE, w. [Cœur, French, heart.] The middle of a stack of hay which has been cut away all round. (Cf. Stump.)

COTTERIL, w. A pot hook; or a hook to hang spits on. (Cf. Pot hanger.)

COUNTABLE. A contraction of unaccountable.

"My missus is countable ornary agin to-day."

COUSINS, e. To call cousins, is to be on intimate terms; but it is generally used in the negative, as, "She and I döant call cousins at all."

COVE.† A lean-to, or low building with a shelving roof. Pigeon-cotes are frequently called pigeon coves in East Sussex.

CRACKLING.S. w. Crisp cakes.

CRANK, CRANKY, e. Merry; cheerful; also drunk.

CRAP, or CRAPGRASS. Ray-grass. Lollum perenne.

CRAY-RING, m. The ring on the top of the long handle of a scythe into which the blade is fixed.

CRAZY. Out of order; dilapidated An old decayed building is said to be crazy. A crazy craft is one un-seaworthy.

CRAZY-HOUSE. A lunatic asylum.

CREEPERS, m. Low pattens mounted on short iron stumps instead of rings.

CRIP, or CRUP. Crisp. Short. Paths are 'crupping up' when frost makes them feel crisp and crunchy under-foot.

"It's going to freeze hard to night because the grass is crup already."

CRISSCROSS [CHRIST'S CROSS], m. The alphabet; so called because in the old horn books it was preceded by a cross.

In the north of England a criss-cross is the mark of a person who cannot write his name.

CROCK, e. A smut or smudge.

"You have got a crock on your nose."

CROCK. [Crocca, Ang. Sax., a pitcher.] An earthen vessel.

"Go to the end of the rainbow and you'll find a crock of gold." – Sussex Proverb.

The Bavarians have a similar proverb; but they say that the crock can only be found by one who was born on a Sunday, and that if such a person can find it and retain it in his possession, it will always contain three ducats.

CROCK BUTTER, m. Salt butter, which in Sussex is usually potted down in brown earthenware crocks.

CROFT, m. [Croft, Ang. Sax., a small enclosed field.] A small piece of pasture-land near to a house.

CROSS-WAYS. A place where four roads meet. That is; where two roads cross one another directly.

CROWNATION. Coronation.

"I was married the day the Crownation was, when there was a bullock roasted whole up at Furrel (Firle) Park. I döant know as ever I eat anything so purty in all my life; but I never got no further than Furrel cross-ways all night, no more didn't a good many."

CROWSFOOT. The butter-cup. Ranunculus bulbosus and allied species.

CRUMMY. Fat, fleshy.

"He aint near so crummy as what he was afore he went tó Lewes jail."

CRUTCHES, e. [Cruche, French, a pitcher.] Broken pieces of crockery.

CRY, e. Several dogs of all kinds.

"I knew it was Miss Jane, by reason she'd got the cry with her."

CUCKOO-FAIR. Heathfield fair, held on April 14th. The tradition in East Sussex is that an old woman goes to Heathfield fair, and there lets the cuckoo out of a bag.

In Worcestershire the saying is that the cuckoo is never heard before Tenbury fair (April 21st), or after Pershore fair (June 26th).

With this may be compared the following German legend, given by Grimm in his "Deutsche Mythologie," p. 691:– "Our Lord was one day passing a baker's shop, when, feeling hungry, He sent in one of His disciples to ask for a loaf; the baker refused it, but his wife, who with his six daughters was standing at a little distance, gave him the loaf secretly, for which good deed they were placed in heaven as seven stars – the Pleiades; but the baker was changed into a cuckoo, which sings from St. Tiburtius' Day

(April 14) to St. John the Baptist's Day (June 24), that is, as long as the seven stars are visible."

CUCKOO GATE, m. A gate which shuts upon two posts which are connected with curved bars, so constructed that only one person can conveniently pass through at a time, and for this reason called in Hampshire a kissing-gate.

And so called in Sussex because you face back to your fellow companion, or because you can corner her in the gate. Also called "To-she-and-fro-she-gate."

CUCKOO'S BREAD AND CHEESE TREE, m. The whitethorn (or hawthorn).

"When the cuckoo comes to the bare thorn, Sell your cow and buy your corn." – Old proverb.

It is very remarkable that this name should be given to the white thorn, as among all Aryan nations this tree is associated with the lightning, while the cuckoo is intimately connected with the lightning gods, Zeus and Thor.

CULLS, or CULLERS. m. The inferior sheep of a flock, culled from the rest and offered for sale in a lot by themselves.

CULVER. A pigeon or dove. This name is retained in the name of a field at Selmeston, which is called the culver ake (the pigeon's oak). And at Culver House, Lancing.

CURIOUS, e. Unsteady; drunk.

"Döant sit so curious when you're swinging, or you'll fall out."

CURMUDGEON, w. To mend up old clothes. A curmudgeon originally meant a hard-bargainer, a miserly fellow, and probably this meaning of the word is connected with mending up rags in a miserly manner.

CUSS. Surly: shrewish.

CUTS, w.† The cross-beams on the floor of a wagon.

CUTTY, m. A wren; also called a kitty, juggy and scutty. These words are sometimes used with the word 'wren' and some times alone.

CUT YOUR STICK. Be off.

This expression is either simply equivalent to a recommendation to prepare a staff in readiness for a journey; or it may be connected with the old way of reckoning by notches or tallies on a stick, and so imply a settlement of accounts before departure.

D

DAB. The sea-flounder.

DALLOP, m. A parcel of tea packed for smuggling, weighing from six to sixteen pounds, or Dollop which generally weighed 2-3 lb, but a Bag (of tea) weighed 5 lb.

DALLOP. A clumsy, shapeless lump of anything tumbled about in the hands.

DANG or DANNEL. Substitutions for damn.

DAPPEN, m. By the time; or perhaps an abbreviation of "should it happen."
"Dappen I've done this job I'll come and lend yer a hand."

DARKS, m. A word used by sailors, but more particularly by smugglers, to signify those nights when the moon does not appear.
In former times, everyone in the agricultural districts of Sussex within reach of the coast was more or less connected with smuggling. The labourer was always ready to help whenever the darks favoured "a run"; the farmer allowed his horses to be borrowed from his stable; the parson (certainly at Selmeston) expressed no surprise at finding tea and tubs buried in the churchyard vaults; the squire asked no questions; the excisemen compounded with the smugglers, and when a difficulty arose as to price, and hard blows were struck, the doctor bound up the wounds for nothing, and made no enquiry as to the dallops of tea or kegs of French brandy, which from time to time were found mysteriously deposited on his doorstep at daybreak.

DARLING, or DAWLIN, m. The smallest pig of a litter; an unhealthy child

DEAD ALIVE. Dull; heavy; stupid.

DEAD HORSE, e. To work for a dead horse is to labour for wages already received, or to work out an old debt.

DEAL. m. The nipple of a sow.

DEARED. Deafened.
"I was amost deared, they made such a noise."

DEATH, m. Deaf. It is rather startling to be told that a person is afflicted with deathness.

DEE, and TO-DEE. Day, and to-day.

DEEDILY, e. Earnestly.
"You was talking so deedily that I didn't like to interrupt you."

DEEDY. Clever; industrious. Efficient ... as a 'deedy stroke' or a 'deedy shot.' Notable.

DEESE, e., or Dee. A place where herrings are dried, now more generally called a herring-hang, from the, fish being hung on sticks to dry.

DEEVE. Dive. The pronunciation of the i like that of the French i is very common in Sussex.

DENIAL, m. A hindrance.
"His deathness is a great denial to him."

DENSHER PLOUGH, m.
[Devonshire Plough?] An instrument used for turf-cutting.

DENTICAL, m. Dainty. Picksome.
"My master says that this here Prooshian (query, Persian?) cat what you gave me is a deal too

Old Shoreham Bridge

dentical for a poor man's cat; he wants one as will catch the meece and keep herself."

DEVIL. This word scarcely ought to have a place in a dictionary of the Sussex dialect, for the country people are very careful indeed to avoid using it. The devil is always spoken of as he, with a special emphasis.

"In the Downs there's a golden calf buried; people know very well where it is – I could show you the place any day. Then why döant they dig it up? Oh, it is not allowed; he would not let them. Has anyone ever tried? Oh, yes, but it's never there when you look, he moves it away."

DEZZICK, m. A day's work.

"I aint done a dezzick for the last six months."

DICK. [Dic. Ang. Sax., a trench] . A ditch.

DIGHT. [Dihtan, Ang. Sax., to prepare.] To adorn; to dress.

"She is gone upstairs to dight up."

DIMSEL, e. A piece of stagnant water, larger than a pond and smaller than a lake.

DISHABILL. [Déshabillé, French, an undress.] Disorder.

"My house is not fit for you to come in, for we're all of a dishabill."

DISH OF TONGUES. A scolding.

"He'll get a middlin' dish of tongues when his mistus comes to hear an't."

DISHWASHER. The water-wagtail. Also called Molly Dishwasher in West Sussex.

DISREMEMBER, m. To forget.

"I can't think of his name; I do disremember things so."

DISSIGHT, m. An unsightly object.

DOBBIN. Sea-gravel mixed with sand. A primitive concrete.

DOBBS, or MASTER DOBBS, e. A kind of brownie or house-fairy who does all sorts of work for

47

members of the family. "Master Dobbs has been helping you," is a common expression to use to a person who has done more work than was expected.

DODDLE. To wag, tremble; walk infirmly.

DODDLEGRASS. Briza media, or quaking grass, called in the north "doddering dock."

DODDLISH. Infirm.

"Old Master Packlebury begins to get very doddlish."

DOG, m. An instrument used by thatchers, to carry straw up the stack. Normally a natural forked branch about four feet long.

DOGS. Small rests for logs in the old open hearths, the top or ornamental part of which very often had the head of a dog on it.

DOG-TIRED. Completely wearied out.

"Oh, master, master, I have watched so

Almshouse at Petworth

long that I am dog-weary." – Taming of the Shrew, Act iv. sc. 2.

DOLE, [Dæl, Ang. Sax., a portion.] Gifts; alms distributed on St. Thomas' day. December 21.

DOLES, m. The short handles on the snethe of a scythe.

DOLING, e. A fishing boat with two masts, each carrying a sprit-sail. Described in Boy's History of Sandwich as "Ships for the King's use furnished by the Cinque Ports."

DOLLERS. The people who go round gathering doles. I.e., the alms.

DOLPHIN. A fly which attacks beams.

DONE-OVER. Tired out; a transposition of overdone, in the same way as go-under is always used for under-go.

DOOLE. A conical lump of earth, about three feet in diameter at the base, and about two feet in height, raised to show the bounds of parishes or farms on the Downs.

DOSSES or DORSELS, e. Panniers in which fish are carried on horse-back.

DOUT, e. [Do out]. To extinguish the light of a candle.

DOUTERS. Instruments like snuffers, used for extinguishing a candle without cutting the wick.

DOWELS, e. Levels; low marshes in which the water lies in winter and wet seasons.

DOWN. Laid up by illness.

"He's down with a bad attack of brown crisis on the chest, least-ways that's what the doctor calls it."

DOWN-BED. A bed on the floor. Or a shake-down, a temporary bed.

DOZZLE. A small quantity.

"He came in so down-hearted that I couldn't be off from giving him a dozzle of victuals, and I told him if he could put up with a down-bed, he might stop all night."

DRACLY-MINUTE. (From dracly, directly, and this minute.) Immediately.

"Ye be to goo dracly-minute."

DRAGGLE- TAIL. A slut.
"Dame Durden kept five serving
    maids
To carry the milking pail,
'Twas Doll and Bet and Sall and Kate,
And Dorothy-draggle-tail."

DRAINING-SPOON, w. An iron tool used by drainers to take out the earth which crumbles down to the bottom of the cutting.

DRAUGHT. A drawing.

"There was a gentleman making a draught of the church this morning."

DRAUGHT. 61 lbs., or a quarter of a pack of wool (240 Ibs.), with one pound allowed for the turn of the scale.

DRAW. A stratagem or device whereby a person is caught or drawn as it were into a trap.

DRAY, or DRAW. A squirrel's nest. A drey.

On St. Andrew's day, November 30, there was in former times an annual diversion called squirrel hunting, when crowds of people went out into the woods with sticks and guns, with which they not only destroyed squirrels, but anything that came in their way. This custom was kept up in Sussex till within the last fifty years, but now, in consequence of the inclosure of coppices and more strict preservation of game, it is wholly discontinued. (*Parish was writing about 1870.*)

DREAN, m. A drain.

DREDGE. A mixture of oats and barley, now very little sown.

DREDGE, m. [Dræge, Ang. Sax., a drag.] A quantity of bushes, chiefly of thorn, bound together and drawn over meadows for the purpose of pulverizing dung or mould, called also a bush harrow.

DRIB. [Dripan, Ang. Sax., to drop.] A very small quantity of anything.

DRIFTWAY, m. [Drifan, Ang. Sax., to drive.] A cattle-path to water; a way by which sheep or cattle are driven, generally a greenway from high ground to low.

DRILLATY, m. [Corruption of dilatory.]

DRINK, m. Medicine for cattle.
"I gave the old cow a drink last night, and she's up again and looking eversmuch better this morning."

DRINKER ACRE, e. The land set apart on dividing brook-land (which was depastured in common) for mowing, to provide drink and provisions for the tenants and labourers.

DROPHANDKERCHIEF.   The game of kiss-in-the-ring.

DROVE-ROAD. An unenclosed road through a farm leading to different fields. Especially, to the tenantry down in the manor.

DRUGGED, e. Half dried; said of linen, etc.

DRUV. Driven. "I wunt be druv" is a favourite maxim with Sussex people. In the shortened form, "Wunt be druv" has now become the motto of the county.

DRYTHE. [Drugath, Ang. Sax.] Drought. Thirst.
"Dry the never yet bred dëarth." – Sussex proverb.

DUBBY, e. Short; blunt.
"I be dubersome whether she'll ever make a needlewoman, her fingers be so dubby."

DUBERSOME, m. Doubtful. This Anglo-Saxon form of termination is not uncommon in Sussex; we find it in timersome for timid, wearisome, and other words.

DUFF. This word, which is evidently only a variation of dough, is used for a pudding made with no other ingredients but flour and water; sometimes called hard dick.
Plum duff is the same with currants.

DUFFER, e. A pedlar. This word is applied only to a hawker of women's clothes.

DUMBLEDORE, w. The humble bee. Or bumble bee.

DUNCH, w. Deaf; slow of comprehension. Dunny.

DUNG-CART RAVES, w. A framework fitted on to a cart to accommodate an extra load.

DUNNAMANY, m. I do not know how many.
"There was a dunnamany people come to see that gurt hog of mine when she was took bad, and they all guv it in as she was took with the information. We did all as ever we could for her. There was a

bottle of stuff what I had from the doctor, time my leg was so bad, and we took and mixed it in some warm milk and give it her lew warm, but naun as we could give her didn't seem to do her any good."

DUNNAMUCH, m. I do not know how much.

"She cost me a dunnamuch for sharps and pollard and one thing and t'other."

DUP, e. To walk quickly.

"You was dupping along so, I knew you was late."

DUTCH COUSINS, e. Great friends. This expression is only used along the coast.

"Yes, he and I were reg'lar Dutch cousins; I feels quite lost without him."

DWAIRS, m. Strong cross-bars in the floor of a waggon. The one in the centre is called the fore-dwair, the one at the back, the hind dwair. They are also called the cuts.

East Lavant

E

EARS.† The irons to which the bail of a bucket is fastened

EARSH, w. A stubble field; as a wheat earsh, a barley earsh – frequently pronounced ash.

EARTH. To turn up the ground as a mole does. Or to lodge as a badger does.

EDDEL. [Ang. Sax., adl, corrupted.] Rotten.

EELSHEAR, e, or EELSPEAR. An iron instrument with three or four points, fastened to the end of a long pole, 8 to 10 feet, by means of which it is thrust into muddy ponds and ditches for the purpose of catching eels.

E'EN-A'MOST. [Corruption of even almost.] Nearly.

" 'Tis e'en-a'most time you gave over eelshearing for this year."

EFFET, m. [Efete, Ang. Sax.] A newt or eft. Often pronounced affut. Dry efts are those found in the earth under hedge banks, and are said by the country people to be poisonous.

EGG. [Eggian, Ang. Sax., to excite.] To urge on; to incite.

"They egged him on to fight."

ELDERN. Made of elder.

ELEVENER, w. (Generally said Levener or Leveneses.) A

Chanctonbury Ring

luncheon.

In Durham the haymakers and reapers call their afternoon meal in the field their "four o'clock."

ELLAR and ELLET, e. [Elarn, Ang. Sax.] The elder tree.

ELLEM and ELVEN, m. [Ellm, Sax.] The elm. (Elven = made of elm wood.)

ELLER. The alder tree.

ELYNGE, m. [Ellende, Ang. Sax., foreign.] Solitary; far from neighbours; uncanny; eerie.

" 'Tis a terrible ellynge lonesome old house, and they do say as how there's a man walks under them gurt elven trees o'nights, but I've never seen him myself."

END-ON, e. In a great hurry.

"He went at it end on, as though he meant to finish afore he begun."

ENEW. Enough.

ERNFUL. Sad; lamentable.

ETHER, or EDDER. [Ang. Sax., ether, edor.] A hedge. A piece of pliant underwood, wound between the stakes of a new-made hedge.

"An eldern stake and blackthorn ether
Will make a hedge to last for ever."

EYED-AND-LIMBED, m. "He eyed and limbed me" means, he anathematized my eyes and limbs.

Rodmell

F

FAD. A whim.

FADDY. Fanciful.

FAG, w. To cut corn or stubble close to the ground.

FAGGING-HOOK or FAG-HOOK, m. A hook or bill fastened on a long stick for trimming hedges, or for fagging corn.

FAGOT, m. A good-for-nothing girl. A baggage.

"I know I'm a saucy little fagot" – A patient to her doctor.

FAGOT-ABOVE-A-LOAD, e. Rather too much of a good thing. "Well, I do call it a fagot-above-a-load, to have to go down to Mr. Barham's twice a day."

FAIL. To fall ill; generally used of catching complaints.

"He looks to me very much as though he was going to fail with the measles."

FAIRY-RINGS. Circles of grass which are higher, and of a deeper green than the grass which grows round them; attributed to the dancing of the fairies.

"Ye elves – you demi-puppets, that by moonshine do the green sour ringlets make, whereof the ewe not bites." – Tempest, Act v. sc. 1.

FAIRY-SPARKS, e. Phosphoric light seen on various substances in the night-time.

FALL, m. The autumn.

"I have the ague every spring and fall."

FALL. [Feallan, Ang. Sax.] To cut down timber.

"These trees are getting too thick, I shall fall a few of them next year."

FAN, e. To banter; to tease. Also to beat or thrash one.

"Be not angry, most mighty princess, that I have adventured to try your taking of a false report. ... The love I bear him
Made me to fan you thus; but the Gods made you
Unlike all others, chaffless. Pray you pardon." – Cymbeline, Act i. sc. 7.

FANER, w., or FANNER-HAWK. A hawk.

FARE. § [An old English word, probably connected with the German fahren, and Dutch vaer.] A period during which certain kinds of fishing took place; as shotnet-fare, tucknet-fare, cock-fare, etc. (F. S. Sawyer from the Brighton Custumal, 1580.)

FARISEES. [Fairieses.] Fairies. By an unfortunate use of the re-duplicated plural, the Sussex country people confuse the ideas of fairies and Pharisees in a most hopeless manner. A belief in fairies is by no means extinct in the South Downs districts, and among other stories the following was most seriously told me,—

"I've heard my féather say, that when he lived over the hill, there was a carter that worked on the farm along wid him, and no one couldn't think how t'was that this here man's horses looked so much better than what any one else's did. I've heard my féather say that they was that fat that they couldn't scarcely get about; and this here carter he was just as much puzzled as what the rest was, so cardinley he laid hisself up in the stáable one night, to see if he could find the meaning an't.

"And he hadn't been there very

Sedilia and tombs of Gervase and Stephen Alard, Winchelsea

long, before these here liddle farisees they crep in at the sink hole; in they crep; one after another; liddle tiny bits of chaps they was, and each an 'em had a liddle sack of corn on his back as much as ever he could carry. Well! in they crep, on they gets, up they clims, and there they was, just as busy feeding these here horses; and prensley one says to t'other, he says, 'Puck.' says he, 'I twets, do you twet?' And thereupon, this here carter he jumps up and says, 'Dannel ye,' he says, 'I'll make ye twet afore I've done wudye!' But afore he could get anigh 'em they was all gone, every one an 'em.

"And I've heard my féather say, that from that day forard this here carter's horses fell away, till they got that thin and poor that he couldn't bear to be seen along wid 'em, so he took and went away, for he couldn't abear to see hisself no longer; and nobody aint seen him since."

FAT-HEN. The plant chenopodium album; called also goosefoot.

FAVOUR, m. To resemble; a resemblance.
Duke Sen: "I do remember in this shepherd boy some lively touches of my daughter's favour."
Orla: "My Lord, the first time that I ever saw him methought he was a brother of your daughter." – As You Like It, Act v. sc. 4.

FAY. To prosper; to go on favourably.
"It fays well," sounds as if it was closely connected with il fait bien.

FEGS. An exclamation.
"Why! you are smart, fegs! "

FESTICAL, e. [Corruption of Festival.] A feast.
"There ain't agoing to be any school festical to-year."

FETCH. A trick; a stratagem; a

55

false appearance.
"Mere fetches; the images of revolt and flying off." King Lear. Act ii. sc. 4.

FID. To work too hard at anything. In Yorkshire the word foy has the same meaning.

FIGHT. To flog. A standing complaint of parents against a school-teacher is, "I wants more learning and less fighting."

FILE. A cunning, deceitful person. In the same sense the word is used in speaking of a hare running her file.

FILL-DICK, m. The month of February.
"February fill the dick,
Every day white or black."
– Sussex proverb.

FIRE-FORK, w. An iron prong for raking ashes out of the oven.

FIRE-SPANNEL, m. A lazy person, who is always sitting by the fireside.

FIRM, m. A form; a bench without a back.

FISHERMEN. Along the South Coast fishermen have nicknames.
Hastings: Chop backs. (From an ancient affray.)
Eastbourne: Willicks, willickers. (Guillemots.)
Seaford: Shags. (Cormorants.)
Brighton: Jugs.
Worthing: Pork bolters.

FITCHES. Vetches.

FITTING, m. Proper; right.
"I didn't think it was at all fitting that he should call me over, and bellick about house same as he did, just because his supper wasn't ready dracly minute."

FITTY. Subject to fits.
The following extract from the Selmeston parochial account book shows how afflicted persons were dealt with in former times, –
"Ladiday, 1790. This is an agreement which is between the Church wardens and Overseers and Parishioners of the Parish of Selmeston, in the County of Sussex.
"The said parishioners do agree that R. Hillman should take Jas. Norman at two shillings and six-pence per week so long as he continues in the fitty state, but when Mr. Hillman shall give it in that he can work well, and equal with other boys, he, the said Hillman, will do and keep him, the said boy, for as little and little money as any parishioner shall think proper."

FLAKE, e. Cleft wood. Flaking is making the flakes into hurdles very close and longer than folding hurdles and used for garden shelter, etc.

FLAM, w. A small net used in ferritting to cover the rabbit-holes. The net is made into a bag shape.

FLAP, w. A large broad mushroom.

FLAP JACK. A sort of tart made of apples baked without a pan, in a thin piece of paste; also called apple turnover.

FLAPPERS, e. Pieces of wood which the fishermen strap over their boots when they walk on the shingle.

FLAPPERS. Young wild ducks which have just taken to the wing but are unable to fly.

FLASKET, w. [Fflasget, Welsh, a shallow basket.] A clothes basket; a shallow washing tub.

FLAT, m. A hollow in a field. Also low-lying water meadows.

"The water lays so in these flats."

FLAW, m. To strip bark; to flay. Called also Rining.

"He's got a job of tan-flawing."

FLECK, m. FLICK, or FLOX. [Flys, Ang. Sax., fleece; down.] The fur of hares or rabbits.

"A pillowbedde stuffed with fflox." – Inventory, 1549.

"Old Mus Crackshott left two robbuts down at our house when he come to fetch his rent o' Saddaday. Purty much knocked about they was – so my mistus she put 'em into a pudden for Sunday, but when we come to set down to dinner they'd biled theirselves all away, and all the robbut as we could find was fower ounces of duck shot and some liddle bits of fleck for flavouring! and I says to my mistus, I says, 'If these be Mus Crackshott's robbuts I'd as lief have brencheese.' "

FLEED. [Fléche, French.] The inside fat of a hog before it is melted into lard.

FLEED-CAKES. Cakes made with fresh fleed: an indispensable adjunct to the family festival of pig-killing.

FLEET, e. To be set afloat.

A vessel is said to fleet when the tide flows sufficiently to enable her to move.

FLEW.† [Flouw, Vlouw, Dutch.] A kind of fishing net.

FLIGHT. To go to flight (or to go

Church Street, Steyning

flitting) is to shoot wild ducks, woodcocks or plover at twilight.

"There was three of our chaps went out t'other day evening purty nigh up as fur as Laughton to flight; but all as ever they brought home along wid 'em was Master Pelts, the shoe maker, as had gone up on the quiet two hours afore, and laid hisself up along wid a gurt bottle of whiskey; and when they got up to the brooks there he was a layin' on his back and a hollerin' of hisself hoarse, and shootin' up in the air at the rooks a-going over to Furrel, till they was forced to take his gun away from him and carry him home."

FLINDERMOUSE, e; FLITTER-MOUSE, m.; FLIT, or FLUTTER-MOUSE. w. A bat.

FLIT, m. or FLEET. Shallow; thin. When water is low it is said to be flit; and land is flit when there is only a slight layer of good earth upon it.

FLIT,c. [Flet, Ang. Sax., cream.] A milk skimmer.

FLIT, e. A bat. Also called flinder-mouse.
A bat coming indoors is considered an evil omen.

FLIT-MILK. Skim milk.

FLOG, m. To tire; to be wearied out.
"I was fairly flogged by the time I got home."

FLOUNDERS. Animals found in the livers of rotten sheep; also called flooks.

FLOUSH-HOLE. [Fluissen, Dutch, to flow fast.] A hole which receives the waste water from a mill pond.

FLOWER. [Corruption of Floor.] Pronounced flöwer.

FLOWN-IN, e. To be overtaken by the tide.
"You're too oudacious daring on they sands; if you döánt mind you'll be flown in, one of these days."

FLUE. [Flaauw, Dutch, weak, feeble.] Delicate; a flue horse is one which always looks thin, and will not carry flesh.

FLUSH, e. Swampy; as ground after a continuance of wet weather.

FLUTTERGRUB, m. A man who takes a delight in working about in the dirt, and getting into every possible mess.

FLUX, e. To snatch at anything; to blush.

FLY GOLDING, e. The ladybird. (See Bishop Barnaby.) Also God Almighty's cow, Lady Anne and Ladycow.

FOB, e. To froth as beer does.

FOB, e. The froth of beer; the foam on a horse's mouth. Sea froth.

FOG, w. Long grass growing in pastures in late summer or autumn, not fed down, but allowed to stand through the winter. Same meaning as Fag.

FOLDING-BAR, w. An iron bar used for making the holes in which the wattles are fixed for folding the sheep.

FOLD-TARE, or FOLD-TAIL, m. The improvement of land caused by sheep having been folded on it.

FOOTY. Silly; foolish; worthless. Little.
"Just a footy dozzle " just a small drink.

FORCED. Obliged.

"I was forced to putt on my spartacles."

FORDROUGH, e. A cattle-path to water; a grass ride. A drove or drift-way.

FORE, m. Front. In Yorkshire the spring is called "the fore-end of the year."

FORECAST, m. Forethought.

FORE-DOOR, m. The front door.

FORE-HORSE, m. "He has got the fore-horse by the head" is a Sussex expression for "he has got matters well in hand."

FOREIGNER. A stranger; a person who comes from any other county but Sussex.

At Rye, in East Sussex, that part of the parish which lies out of the boundary of the corporation, is called the Foreign of Rye.

I have often heard it said of a woman in this village, who comes from Lincolnshire, that "she has got such a good notion of work that you'd never find out but what she was an English woman, without you was to hear her talk."

FORERIGHT. Plain spoken; rude; obstinate.

"I döánt know whatever I shall do with that boy, he's so foreright, and he döánt seem to have no forecast of nothing."

FORE-SUMMER, w. The top rail in front of a waggon.

The corresponding rail at the back is called the hawk.

FORNICATE, m. To dawdle; to waste time.

FORREP-LAND, w. (Forest, Old French, a forest.) Used in the manor of Bosham for assart land, or land from which the wood or forest has been cut down, to bring it into cultivation.

FORSTALL, or FOSTEL, m. [Ang. Sax., fore, before; and steal, a stall, place or stead] the house and home buildings of a farm with waste land attached.

FOTHER. To feed cattle.

FOUNDLE, m. Anything found.

"I picked up a foundle yesterday, as I was coming home off the hill."

FOURTHROWS, or FOUR-WENTS, e. A place where four roads meet.

FRAIL, m. Flail.
"Dame Durden kept, five serving men
To use the spade and frail."

FRAYEL, m. (or frail). A flexible basket made of bulrushes, commonly used for packing game.

FRENCHY, e. A foreigner of any country who cannot speak English, the nationality being added or not, as the case seems to require; thus an old fisherman, giving an account of a Swedish vessel which was wrecked on the coast a year or two ago, finished by saying that he thought the French Frenchys, take 'em all in all, were better than the Swedish Frenchys, for he could make out what they were driving at, but he was all at sea with the others.

FRESH, m. Home-brewed small beer, which must be drunk while new or fresh.

FRESH, e. To decorate; to renew.

"I freshed up my bonnet with those ribbons you gave me."

FRESH, e. Fresh air.

"It feels very close to you coming in out of the fresh, but Jane she's had her fevers all day, and I dursn't set the window open to let in any fresh, for I was afraid 'twould give her cold."

FRESH. Not quite drunk, but rather noisy.

FRIT, e. Frightened, Frouden, etc.
"I was quite frit to see him so near the water."

FRITH, e. Young underwood; brushwood growing by the side of hedges.

FRORE, w. Frozen. Spencer uses frorne in the same sense.

FROSTBECK, w. A strong handbill for cutting up turnips when they are frozen.

FROUDEN, m; or FROUGHT, w; or FROUGHT'N'D, m. Frightened. Frit.
I met an elderly man one evening going through the churchyard; it was too dark to see who he was, and I passed without speaking. To my surprise he stopped and began shouting as loud as he could; and recognising his voice, I went back to ask him what was the matter. "Oh dear me, sir!" he said,

"is that you? I didn't know it was you, sir, I'm sure I beg your pardon." It was in vain that I enquired why he was making such a dreadful noise; no answer could I get, beyond that he didn't know who it was. So I wished him good night and went on, under the impression that he was drunk; but the matter was explained by his turning back to say, "I beg your pardon, sir, but I hope you döánt think I was frouden! Bless me, no! I was noways frouden, not at all! I'm a man as aint easily frouden at meeting anyone in the churchyard after dark."

FURLONG. A division of tenantry land.
Not the normal furlong (furrow long) of 220 yards, but a term applied to a parcel of land of any size.

FURNAGE, w. A sum formerly paid by the tenants of the lord of the manor for right to bake in his oven.

FUTTICE, e. A weazel. Also called Kime or Kine.

G

GABERDINE, m. A loose frock still worn in Sussex by farm labourers. "My best way is to creep under his gaberdine." – Tempest, Act ii. sc. 2.

GAFFER, m. Abbreviation of grandfather.

GAFFER, m. A master.
  "Gaffer has given me a holiday."

GAG, e. Showery.

GALLEYBIRD, or GALLOWS-BIRD. The Woodpecker. The great green woodpecker, or yaffle. Yaffle, from its cry; gallowsbird for frequenting old gallows or gibbets for maggots, etc.

GALLOWS. (Pronounced gallus.) To die under the gallows is said to be the fate of a person who dies of overwork.

GALORE.* In abundance. This old Celtic word is still in common use in Scotland and Ireland. It has

Ann of Cleves' House, Southover

lately become common generally.

GAMELING, e. [Gamen, Ang. Sax., a game.] Romping about.

GAMMER, m. Abbreviation of grandmother.

GANSE, e. Merriment; hilarity.

GANSING-GAY, e. Cheerful; lively. "Some people said the children would always be interrupting of us if we went to live so near the school, but for my part I likes to hear them, their voices is so gansing gay its quite company to me."

GAP, m. [Geapu, Ang. Sax., a space.]
An opening through the chalk cliffs on the Southdowns leading to the sea, or to a river, as Birling Gap, Copperas Gap, etc. also called a gut.

GAPE SEED.* Something to stare at.
A person staring out of window is said to be sowing gape seed.

GARATWIST,* or GARTWISTED.
Altogether on one side. Also said when seams pucker in sewing patchwork. etc.

GARRETING, w. Small pieces of flint stuck in the mortar courses in building. Also, of ironstone in flintwork.

GASKIN, e. [Gascony] A kind of cherry largely grown in the neighbourhood of Rye, which is called indifferently "geen" or "gaskin," having been brought from France by Joan of Kent when her husband, the Black Prince, was commanding in Guienne and Gascony.
In olden days a Lord of Berkeley finding housekeeping too costly, agreed with the widow of a Kentish nobleman for lodging and maintenance of himself, his wife, her two waiting women, six serving men, and horses for the whole party at £200 a year, but he died before the year was out of eating too many gaskins.

GATE, w. A farmyard.
"Go through the gate," i.e., the farmyard gate.

GAUNT, e. [Geanian, Ang. Sax.] To yawn.

GAY-GROUND, e. A flower garden.
"I likes to have a bit of gay ground under the window for a look out."

GAZELS, e. [Groseiller, a currant tree.] All kinds of berries, but especially black currants.
Gazel tea is a favourite remedy for a cold.

GEAT. [Geat, Ang. Sax., a gate.]
The Anglo-Saxon form of the word is always used in Sussex.

GEE, m. To get on well with a person.
"We've lived up agin one another for a good many years, and we've always geed together very nicely."

GEEMANY, m. [Corruption of of Gemini!]
"Geemeny! you do mean to be spicy."

GEEN, e. [Guienne, French.] (See Gaskin.

GEE-WOOT. An expression used by waggoners to make the leading horse go to the off side; to the shaft horse the word for the same purpose is hoot. To woot is the contrary command . . . to ease off to the left or near side, or towards the teamster.

GENERALLY-ALWAYS and MOST

GENERALLY ALWAYS, m.
A superlative form of generally.
"My master generally-always comes home none the better for what he's had of a Saddaday night."

GENTLEMAN, m. A person who does not earn his own living. Anyone who is disabled from work. The term is sometimes applied to a sick woman, or even to a horse. "I'm sure I've done all I could for mother; if she isn't a gentleman I should like to know who is!"

GIFTS. White specks which appear on the finger nails, supposed to indicate the arrival of a present.
"A gift on the thumb, is sure to come;
A gift on the finger is sure to linger."

GIFTY w. [Giftig, Dutch.] Unwholesome; poisonous.
"The house smelt quite gifty like."

GIGGLESOME. Given to giggle.

GIMSY, e. Smartly dressed

GIVE-IN. To state an opinion.
"Master Cockleshaw he gives it in that we shall have a change of weather before many days."

GIVE-OVER. Leave off.
"You just give over messing-about among my cabbages."

GLINCY [Glincer, Old French, to slide.] Smooth; slippery; applied to ice.

GLUM. [Glom, Ang. Sax., gloom.] Gloomy.
"The weather looks very glum this morning."

GNANG, e. [Gnagan, Ang. Sax., to gnaw.] To gnash the teeth.

GOAD, e. Any long stick. Pronounced góád.

GOBBET. [Gobet, French, a hasty meal.] A large mouthful of anything; a lump. A small gob.
"Meet I an infant of the house of York,
Into as many gobbets will I cut it,
As wild Medea young Absyrtus did."
– II HENRY VI, Act v. sc. 2.

GOLD CUP. The meadow ranunculus.
The Butter cup. (R. acris, R. bulbosus and R. repens without discrimination.)

GOLE. [Gole, Old French, the gullet. A wooden drain pipe. In the north of England the word is used for a small stream.

GOODEN, or GOODENING, or GOODERS. The custom of going from house to house for doles on St. Thomas's day (21st December). This was done by women only, and a widow had a right to a double dole; the presumed object being to obtain money or provisions for the enjoyment of the approaching festival of Christmas.

GOODMAN. An old title of address to the master of the house. I find the following entries in a book of accounts of the parish of Selmeston, –
1745, December ye 22
"Goodman Casson
payd fower men for Carring John Casson to the ground   00-04-00
payd Tho. Furden for buring John Casson   00-02-06
payd for laying John Casson foarth and one shilling for ather Daved" (affidavit)   00-03-00

GOODY. The title of an elderly widow.
Expences for the yeare 1743:
Payd Goody Gorge for washing and mending her suns cloath and Goody Pumphrey   01-00-06

GOSSIP, e. [Godsibb, Ang. Sáx., a

sponsor.] This word is still used, though very rarely, by old people. "They've brought a child to be christened, but they haven't got no gossips."

GO-UNDER. Undergo.

"The doctor says he must go to the hospital and go under an operation."

GRABBY; e. Grimy; filthy; dirty.

GRAFF, or GRAFFING-TOOL, m.,

GRAFT. or GRAFTER. [Grafan, Ang. Sax., to dig.] A curved spade, generally made of wood shod with iron. Used by drainers. It is narrow and long in shape.

GRANDFATHER, m. A daddy-long-legs.

GRANDMOTHER'S NIGHTCAP. † The white campion. L. dioica.

GRATTEN, m. A stubble field. A rough fallow field which was at first an earsh.

Boxgrove Priory Church

GRATTEN. [Gratter, French, to scratch.] To scratch for the grain that may be left on the grattens.

"By the time the pigs have been grattening for a week they'll look eversmuch better."

GREW, e. A greyhound. A Long dog.

"T'old grew guv Mus' Reynolds a tidy grib."

GREYBEARDS, m. Earthen jugs formerly used in public-houses for beer, and so called from having on them the face of a man with a large beard. Also called Bellarmines because they are effigies in ridicule of Cardinal Bellarmine the persecutor.

GREYBIRD, m. The Thrush. Properly the Missel Thrush. The Song Thrush is the Brown bird.

GRIB, e. Variation of grip. A sharp bite.

GRIDGEN, m. Grudging; stingy. "If he has anything given him, he's that gridgen that he'll never give away naun an't."

GRIG, e. Merry; happy. "Master Harry he's always so grig."

GRIP. [Groep, Ang. Sax.] A small ditch or drain.

GRIZZLE, m. To fret; to grieve. "I know the child aint well, because she's been grizzling about so all day, and she's never one to grizzle when she's well."

GROM, e. [Grommeler, Dutch, to wallow.] Dirty; to soil or make dirty.

GROOM, m. An instrument used by thatchers for carrying bundles of straw.

GROUT-HEADED. Stupidly noisy.

GRUBBY, e. To make in a mess. "You've grubbied our pinney," means "you have dirtied your pinafore.

GRUMMUT. An awkward boy.

Mr. M. A. Lower states that this word is a corruption of the old French gromet, a diminutive of groom; the cabin-boy of the Cinque Port navy was so called. The condition of the distinguished immunities of those ancient corporations was, that they should provide for the King's use a certain number of ships, and in each ship twenty-one men, with one boy, called a gromet –"

GRYST. [Grist, Ang. Sax., a grinding.] Or grist. A week's allowance of flour for a family. Pronounced with a long y or i. Said now of inferior corn ground for fodder and poultry feed, a common complaint of latter day wind and water millers is "We are only grysting now," meaning only grinding cattle food, not flour.

GUBBER, e. Black mud.

GUDGE, m. To probe. "The doctor came and vaccinated our baby yesterday; nasty man! he just did gudge his poor little arm about."

GUESS-SHEEP, m. Young ewes that have been with the ram and had no lambs; so called because it is doubtful or a matter of guess whether they will ever have lambs.

GULL, w. To sweep away by force of running water; a breach made by a torrent. (Gullywash and Gully, a channel made by running water across a road.)

GULL. A gosling. Young geese in

Near Tarring Neville

Sussex are seldom called goslings. GULL, m. The blossom of the willow; called in Cambridgeshire goslins.

GUMMUT. A lout; a stupid fellow.

GUMPTIOUS, e. Smart; tawdry.

GUN, m. To examine carefully; to con over.

"When I gunned her over a little closer, I soon saw that she was too gumptious by half to be a lady."

GURGISE, w. A fish-pool; lake, or pond.

GURT. [Corruption of great.] Gert.

GUT, m. [Gjota, Icel.; Gota, Ang. Sax., a pourer.] An underground drain for water.

GUTTERDICK, m. A small drain.

" 'Taint no use at all for you to make that 'ere gutterdick, what you wants is a gurt gut."

GYLE. A brewing of beer.

H

HABERN, w. The back of the grate Also the sides or hobs.
"Why, whatever have you been a doing with yourself? Your face is as black as a habern!"

HACK. To cough faintly and frequently.

HACK, w. To rake up hay into thin rows.

HACKER, m. To stutter and stammer.

HACK-HOOK, m. [Haccan, Ang. Sax., to cut.] A curved hook with a long handle, used for cutting peas and tares, or trimming hedges.

HACKLE, m. (Hæcele, Ang. Sax., a garment.] A straw covering placed over beehives.

HAFFER or HARFER. A heifer.
"I leave to Jane, my wife's daughter, an haffer of 2 yerys age." – Will of Thos. Donet, of Burwash, 1542.

HAGRIDDEN, m. To be hagridden is to have the nightmare.

HAGTRACK, m. Circles of coarse green grass seen on the meadows and downs, supposed to be tracks of hags or witches who have danced there at night. They are caused by a fungus.

HAITCH, e. A slight passing shower.

HAITCHY, e. Misty. HALF-BAPTIZED'. Privately baptized.
"If you please, Sir, will you be so good as to half-baptize the baby?" "Oh! certainly; but which half of him am I to baptize?"

HALF-BAPTIZED, e. Silly, foolish.
"You must have been half-baptized to water those flowers when the sun was full on them."

HALF-HAMMER, w. The game of hop-step-and-jump.

HALF-SWING PLOUGH, w. A plough in which the mould-board is a fixture.

HAM. [Ang. Sax., hám; German, heim; English, home.] A level pasture field; a plot of ground near a river. A three-sided grass plot is also called a Ham.
"In the country of the Angles as well as here (in North Friesland) every enclosed place is called a hamm." – Outzen's Glossary of the Frisian Language.

HAMPERY, m. [Possibly from empire, French, decayed.] Out of repair.

HAMWOOD, w., or HAMOOD. [Hame-wood.] Pieces of wood on the collar of a horse to which the traces are fixed. Hames.

HAND, m. To be a hand, is to cause a great deal of trouble.
"I was a terrible hand to mother all the time I was down with the titus- fever."

HANDLE-DISH. m. A bowl with a handle.

HANGER, m. A hanging wood on a hill side.

HANSEL, m; or HACKLE, e. To use anything for the first time. A first handling; the same as Hansel below.

HANSEL, m. [Handsylen, Ang. Sax., a giving into the hands.] The first money received in the morning for the sale of goods. The market women have a custom of kissing the first coin, spitting on it, and putting it in a pocket by itself

Amberley Church

or luck.

HAP, m. Perhaps.

HAPPEN-ALONG, m. To come by chance; to arrive unexpectedly.

"Master Tumptops, he's a man as you'll notice mostly happens-along about anyone's dinner-time."

HAPS, m. [Hæps, Ang. Sax.] Hasp of a door or box.

HARD-DICK. Sussex pudding, made of flour and water only. Also called duff.

HARNESS, m. Temper, humour.

"Master's in purty good harness this morning."

HAROLD. A common Christian name in East Sussex, which is always pronounced the same as the word earl.

HASSOCK, e. [Possibly from Haso, Ang. Sax, dry; rugged.] Anything growing in a thick matted state. A thick wooded shaw or little wood.

HATCH', m. To sicken for any complaint.

"I think she's hatching the measles." This expression seems to correspond very closely with that used by physicians when they

68

speak of the period of incubation.

HATCH, m. (Haccan; Ang Sax., to hack.) To dress the bark of trees.

HATCH. (Hec, Ang. Sax., a gate.) In names of places probably means a gate.

It is usually found on the borders of forests, as Coleman's Hatch, Plaw hatch and Claw-hatch, in Ashdown forest.

HATCH, w. A gate; a half-door.

HATCHEL, w. To rake cut grass into small rows.

HATCHET-PIECES.† Small-pieces of land of irregular shape.

HAULM. [Healm, Ang. Sax.] The straw of beans, peas, tares, etc.

HAUST, m. A place for drying hops.

HAVE, m. To lead or take. To forcibly conduct.

"I shall have him down to his grandmother while I go haying."

HAVILER, or HEAVER, e. [Heafer, Ang. Sax.] A crab. The green or mud crab. Also called Aviller and Jack-aviller.

HAWK, w. See Fore-summer.

HAYWARD, m. [Haw-ward; hedge-ward] An officer of the lord of the manor, whose business it was to look after the hedges and see that the boundaries were kept right.

HEAD, m. "To your head" is the same as "to your face." "I told him to his head that I wouldn't have such goings on in my house any more."

"To the head of Angelo accuse him home and home." – Measure for Measure, Act iv. sc. 2.

HEAD-ACHE, e. The corn poppy. Papaver rhæas.

HEADLANDS, m. The part of the field close against the hedges. In Sussex when ploughing with four yoke oxen the headlands were wider than today because more room was needed to turn the team.

HEADPIECE, m. (Not only local.) The head considered with regard to the intellect.

"He's got a very good head-piece, and if he could have had a little more schooling he'd have made something better than a ploughboy."

HEAK.§ Another name for the flew.

Erredge (History of Brighton) says that in Yorkshire the nets used for fishing in the river Ouse are still called heaks.

HEAL, m. [Hélan, Ang. Sax., to cover or conceal.] To cover. Some-times said as broadly as 'háál.'

"I healed up the roots with some straw." Sometimes expressed as "healing up."

"In the ancient English dialect the word 'hell' was taken in a large sense for the general receptacle of all souls whatsoever, and it is so used in the old translation of the Psalms in our Common Prayer Book (Ps. lxxxix,47), which sense may be confirmed from the primary and original signification of the word; according to which it imports no more than an invisible and hidden place, being derived from the old Saxon word 'hil' which signifies to hide, or from the participle thereof, helled, that is to say, hidden or covered; as in the western parts of England, at this very day, to 'hele' over anything, signifies, amongst the common people, to cover it, and he that covereth an house with tile or slate is called an 'hellier'; whence it appears that the word 'hell,' according to its primitive notion, exactly answers to the Greek 'hades' which signifies the common mansion of departed souls, and was so called because it is an unseen place." – Lord Chancellor King on the Apostle's Creed, pp. 233,193,194. Ed. Lond. 1702.

HEALED. [Hyldan, Ang. Sax., to incline.] When a ship goes over to one side she is said to have healed over

HEALING, m. A coverlet; a counterpane.

In the will of Rev. H. Marshall, he leaves "2 pillowberes and a healing." (... ij pylowbers, a hillyng, ...) The will was dated 9th August, 1550.—S.A.C. XIII. p. 53.)

HEART, m. Condition; said of ground.

"I've got my garden into pretty good heart at last, and if so be as there warnt quite so many sparrs and grey birds and roberts and one thing and t'other, I dunno but what I might get a tidy lot of sass. But there! taint no use what ye do as long as there's so much varmint about."

HEAVE-GATE, m. [Hefan and geat, Ang. Sax.] A low gate, so constructed as to lift out from the posts, instead of opening with hinges. Often pronounced "E-géát." especially in East Sussex.

HEDGE-HOG. Venus' comb. Scandix pecten-veneris. Or Shepherd's needle.

HEDGE-PICK, or HEDGE-MIKE, m. The hedge sparrow: or Dunnock.

HEEN, m. [Hæn, Ang. Sax.] A hen. "I throwed a stone at a liddle hedge-pick a settin' on the heave-géát, and killed Mrs. Pankurstes'

Bodiam Castle

gurt old packled heen." (Packled meaning "Speckled.")

HEGGLING. Vexatious; trying; wearisome.

HEIRS; * Young timber trees.

HELP, m. To give anything into a person's hands.
"I will help the letter to him if You'll write a few lines."

HELVE, e. To gossip.

HELVE, e. A long gossip.

HEM, m. Very.
"Hem crusty old chap our shepherd is surelye! I says to him yesterday, I says, ' 'Tis hem bad weather, shepherd,' I says. 'Ah,' says he, ' 'tis better than no weather at all;' and hem-a-bit would he say any more."

HEM-A-BIT, m. Not a bit; certainly not.

HEMMEL, e. A fold. Connected with the Icelandic word hemja, to restrain. To hem in.

HEMPSHARE, or HEMSHARE.† Certain lands in the centre of Brighton, so named from having been used by persons engaged in the fishing trade for growing hemp for rope making. The word is found in the court rolls. 1660.

HENRIP, w. A hen-coop.

HERE-AND-THERE-ONE.
An expression wed to signify an average or on an average, as "He aint much of a boy I know, but he's quite as good a boy as you'll find here-and-there-one."

HERRING-HANG, e.† A place where herrings are hung up to dry; also called a dee, or a deese.

HIDE. [Hyd, Ang. Sax.] A hide of land is about 120 acres. In Saxon times it meant as much land as could be tilled with one plough; a family possession.

HIGGLER, m. A huckster; so called from higgling over his bargains.
A Horhsam Market Deed of 1756 refers to restrictions on hawkers and higglers.

HIKE, m. To call roughly. To pull out, as root-grubbing, etc.
"He hiked me out of the pew."

HILL, m. The Southdown country is always spoken of as "The hill" by the people in the Weald.
"He's gone to the hill, harvesting."

HILL-UP, m. [Helan, Ang. Sax., to cover.] To hill-up hops is to raise small hills or heaps over the roots for the purpose of keeping them dry in the winter.

HISN, m. His own. His (Not now localised.)
The possessive noun is thus conjugated in Sussex – Mine, thine, hisn or hern. Ourn. yourn, theirn.

HITHER, m. Near. Nearer to some definite position.
"His in the hither croft."

HOBBLE, m. A doubt; an uncertainty.

HOB-LAMB, m. A pet lamb, brought up by hand. Also called a Sock lamb.

HOB-UP. To bring up anything by hand.
A parishioner of mine once came to complain to me that her husband had threatened to ill-use her on account of two little pigs which she was hobbing up; but as I found that his objection rested on the fact that she was hobbing up the pigs so carefully that she

insisted on taking them to bed with her, I declined to interfere.

HOCKLANDS, HOOKLANDS, or OCKLANDS. [Hóh, Ang. Sax., a heel.] Hock-shaped pieces of meadow land.—Leo's Ang. Sax. Names.

HOCK-MONDAY, w. The second Monday after Easter, kept as a festival in remembrance of the defeat of the Danes in King Etheldred's time.

HOE, w. Fuss; anxiety.

"I döánt see as you've any call to putt yourself in no such terrible gurt hoe over it."

HOG-FORM, w. A bench on which pigs are laid to be killed and dressed.

On the knuckle of a pig's fore-leg there are always six marks, about the size of a pea, which are believed to have been caused by the devil's fingers when he entered the herd of swine.

HOGGET, w. A young sheep, just more than a year old.

HOG-JET, w. A small bucket, fastened into a long handle, by which the food is taken out of the hog-tub.

HOGO.* [Haut gout, French.] A strong foul smell. Or any strong flavour accompanied with a powerful smell.

HOGPOUND, m. The pigstye; a favourite rendezvous on Sundays.

"Ah! many's the time as we've stood over the hog-pound together, and looked 'em over, and rackoned 'em up, whiles people was in church; little did he think as he'd be putt in before that hog was killed! and he always allowed

she'd weigh sixty stun." "Putt in" means buried.)

HOLL, e. To hurl; to throw.

HOLLARDS.* Dead branches of trees.

HOLP, m. [Healp, Ang. Sax.] The perfect of help.

"She had me round to the pound, to see a little hogget what she'd hobbed-up; and then she had me indoors and holp me to a cup of tea and some honey-bread "

HOLT, m. [Holt, Ang. Sax., a grove.] A small plantation. Also a wood gap, small and on the side of a hill, or a small plantation, usually alongside a hill, like Clayton Holt.

HOLT. A hold.

" 'Tis just like a lawyer, if once it takes a holt 'an ye, ye doant very easy get free agin."

HOLT, m. [Corruption of Halt.] A call always used to stop a person.

HOLT-SUNDAY, e. Easter-day.

There is a tradition that the sun always dances on the morning of Holy-Sunday, but nobody has ever seen it because the devil is so cunning that he always puts a hill in the way to hide it.

HOME-DWELLERS, m. People accustomed to live in houses, as opposed to tramps.

"A good many of these people who've come harvesting this year, look like home-dwellers."

HONEY-BREAD. Bread and honey.

HOOKE, or Hook. [Hoc, Ang. Sax., a hook.] A name given to several places in Sussex. Often to farms.

HOP-DOG, m. A caterpiller peculiar to the hop gardens.

Gateway, Amberley Castle

HOP-DOG, m. An instrument used to draw the hop-poles out of the ground, for the purpose of carrying them to the bin to be picked. It was attached to a long wooden handle.

HOP-HORSE, e. A short ladder used by the hob-pickers.

HOP-MAND, w. [Mond, Ang. Sax., a basket.] A vessel used in brew-houses.

HORN-FAIR, m. Rough music 'with frying pans, horns, etc., generally reserved for persons whose matrimonial difficulties have attracted the attention of their neighbours. The fair annually held in Charlton, Kent (now abolished), was always known as Horn fair.

HORNICLE, w. A hornet.

HORSEBEACH or HUSBEECH, w. The hornbeam.

HORSE-DAISY, w. The ox-eye daisy. (Chrysthemum leucanthemum.)

HOSTE, e. Described by Durrant Cooper as "A vendor of articles out of shops or houses," so used at Hastings. From the old French word Hoste, which meant both a host and a guest.

This word is used in the second sense, – a guest, a person allowed to come, a stranger.

"Every person not lotting or shotting to the common charge of the Corporation, who should be a common hoste in the fishmarket." – Hastings Corporation Records,

1604.

HOT, m. To warm up.

"I was that cold when I got indoors that gaffer hotted up some beer for me.

HATAGOE.* To move nimbly; spoken of the tongue.

HOT-CHILLS, m. The fever that accompanies the ague.

HOTH, m. Hawth. The name of Hoathly seems connected with this word.

" 'Tis very poor ground, it wont grow naun but heath and hoth."

HOT-POT m Hot ale and spirits.

HOUNDS, w. The part of a wagon to which the fore-wheels and shafts are attached.

HOUSED, e. When hops have a great deal of bine, and the poles are thickly covered over the top, so as almost to shut out the light and sun, they are said to be "housed."

HOUSEL, m. Household goods. Hustlement.

"Whose housel is that up on the wagon?"

HOVELER, e. A pilot. Latterly, an unlicensed pilot.

HOVELERS, e. Men who go out to sea in boats for the purpose of meeting homeward-bound vessels, and engaging with the captain to unload them when they enter the harbour. (Huffler at Shoreham.)

HOVER, m. Light; spoken of the ground or soil. Friable, not clayey.

HOVER, m. Looking cold and shivery.

"Some of the children looked middlin' hover as they went along to school this morning through the snow."

HOVER, m. To hover hops is to measure them lightly into the basket.

HOWK, e. To dig. Possibly connected with the Dutch word houwen, to hew.

HOWLERS, w. Boys who in former times went round wassailing the orchards. A custom now nearly obsolete.

The custom of wassailing used to be observed on the eve of the Epiphany, when the howlers went to the orchards, and there encircling one of the best bearing trees, drank the following toast, –
"Here's to thee, old apple tree,
May'st thou bud, may'st thou blow,
May'st thou bear apples enow!
Hats full! Caps full!
Bushel, bushel, sacks full!
And my pockets full, too! Huzza!"

The wassailers derived their name from the Anglo-Saxon salutation on pledging one to drink, which was wæs hæl, be of health; to which the person pledged replied drinc hæl, I drink your health.

HOWSUMDEVER, m. or HOW-SUMEVER. However.

HOX, w. To cut the hamstrings; to cut the sinew of a rabbit's leg and put the other foot through, in order to hang it up.

HUCK, e. The pod of a pea.

Children get the pods and cry to each other, –
"Pea-pod hucks,
Twenty for a pin;
If you döänt like 'em
I'll take 'em back agin."

HUCK, e. A hard blow or knock rudely given.

HUCK, e. To spread anything about, such as manure.

HUCKLE-BONE, e. The small bone found in the joint of the knee of a sheep, used by children for playing the game of dibs.

Dr. Clarke, in his travels in Russia, 1810, vol. I., p. 177, says, "In all the villages and towns from Moscow to Woronetz, as in other parts of Russia, are seen boys, girls, and sometimes old men, playing with the joint bones of sheep. This game is called dibbs by the English. It is of very remote antiquity; for I have seen it very beautifully represented on Grecian vases, particularly on a vase in the collection of the late Sir William Hamilton, where a female figure appeared most gracefully delineated kneeling upon one knee, with her right arm extended, the palm downwards, and the bones ranged along the back of her hand and arm; a second is in the act of throwing up the bones in order to catch them. In this manner the Russians play the game."

HUCKLE-MY-BUFF, c. A beverage composed of beer, eggs and brandy.

HUCKMUCK. w. A wicker strainer used in brewing. It was 3ft. 2 in. long.

HUFF, e. To scold or take to task.

HUFFY, e. Liable to take offence.

HUGGER-MUGGER, m. In disorder; without system.
"We have done but greenly in hugger-mugger to inter him." – Hamlet, Act iv. sc. 5.

HULL, e. To throw.

HULL, m. [Hulze, Dutch, a shell of a pea; a case.] The husk or chaff of corn; the shell of a nut; the pod of peas.

HULL, w. To shell peas; to strip off the outside covering of anything.

Westham

HUMBLE-COW, e. A cow without horns. Sometimes called a Moiley cow, a muley cow or a not-cow.

HUNCH, m. A nudge.

"I thought they were sweet-hearts, because I see him give her a hunch in church with his elbow."

HUNG-UP, m. Hindered.

"I was so hung up for time all last week I couldn't come."

HURLEY-BULLOO, m. A disturbance.

HURR, m. Tart; rough-tasting.

"The doctor's ordered me to drink some of this here claret wine, but I shall never get to like it, it seems so hurr."

HURST, m. [Hurst, Ang. Sax.] A wood.

HURTS, w. Whortle berries, blae-berries: bilberries: hurtleberries.

HUSS, m. To hiss; to buzz; said of insects.

"The old owl I fancy did huss and spet when I went to take the eggs! and just did scratch a gurt plááce in my harnd wud he's old to-a-nails, too."

HUSS, e. To caress.

The children play a game which is accompanied by a song beginning, –
"Hussing and bussing will not do,
But go to the gate, knock and ring, –
Please, Mrs. Brown, is Nellie within?"

HUSSER-AND-SQUENCHER, e. A pot of beer with a dram of gin in it.

HYPOCRITE, e. A lame person.

This word may be possibly connected with, or a corruption of the old word hippand, meaning limping or hopping.

"Yes, she's a poor afflicted creature; she's quite a hypocrite; she can't walk a step without her stilts."

I

ICE-BONE. The edge-bone of beef. The aitch bone.

ICHON'EM. Each one of them. Each of them.

IDGET, w. A horse hoe; called also a nidget, a Nideot or edget.

ILL-CONDITIONED, m. Ill-tempered

"He's the most ill-conditioned impersome young chap I know; a proper out-and-outener."

ILL-CONVENIENT. m. Inconvenient.

IMPERSOME. e. Impertinent.

IN, w. [Innian, Ang. Sax., to take in.] To inclose land. Also spelt Inn. "I inned that piece of land from the common."

An Anglo-Saxon estate was usually divided into two parts; one of which, called the inland, was occupied by the proprietor with his establishment; and the other, called the útland, was ceded to the servants in return for rent and service, as a reward for their assistance, or as the means of support to those who were not freed-men.

IN, w. To house corn.

"The corn was all inned before Michaelmas day."

ING. [Ing, Ang. Sax.] A common pasture or meadow.

INGENURIOUS, e. Ingenious.

"For my part I consider that King Solomon was a very ingenurious man."

INKHORN, m. Inkstand.

"Fetch me down de inkhorn, mistus; I be g'wine to putt my harnd to dis here partition to Parliament. 'Tis agin de Romans,

Sompting

mistus; for if so be as de Romans gets de upper harnd an us, we shall be burnded, and bloodshedded, and have our Bibles took away from us, and dere'll be a hem set out."

INNARDLY, m. Inaudibly; inwardly.

"This new parson of ours says his words so innardly."

INNINGS, w. Land that has been enclosed from the sea.

INNOCENT, m. Small and pretty. Generally applied to flowers.

INTERRUPT, m. To attack.

This word is used to express all kinds and degrees of assault.

INWARD, m. Silent; reserved. Usually said "Innard."

"I can't abear going to work along ud Master Meopham, he be so inward"

INWARDS, or INNARDS. Intestines. Also internal organs.

A story is told in the neighbourhood of Rye of an old man who informed the clergyman after he had been preaching about veracity, that he thought his a capital good sermon, but he did not know what he meant by saying so much about the innards of a hog.

ITEM.* A hint.

ITEM. A dose.

"If I didn't take them little items I was sure to be bad."

IX. [Ex, Ang. Sax., an axis.] An axle tree.

Framfield

J

JACKET, m. To flog or dust his jacket; i.e. beat the dust out of it with him inside.

"I'll jacket him when he comes in."

JACKETTING, m. A hard day's work.

JACKETTING. A scolding.

JACK-HEARN, m. A heron; always spoken of as "a gurt old jack-hearn."

"Parham Park, in West Sussex, can still boast of one of the most interesting heronries in the south of England"
– Knox's Ornithological Rambles in Sussex.

JACK-IN-PRISON, e. Nigella damas cena. Love-in-a-mist.

JACK-IN-THE-HEDGE, e. Lychnis diurna. Red Campion.

JACK-UP, m. To give up anything in a bad temper.

A man came to my house by himself one Christmas Eve to sing carols, and at the end of each line he stopped to explain why the other singers were absent. He began, –
"While Shepherds watched their flocks by night." "If you please, sir, my party's all jacked up" – "All seated on the ground" – "Yes, sir, there was young Harry down here, and my brother Jem, and Tom and George, we've all been a practising together, and now they're properly jacked up" (and so on to the end of the hymn.)

JAMBREADS, m. Slices of bread and jam. Sussex folk say brencheese, brenbutter, but never brenjam; always jambread and always honey-bread.

JANUARY-BUTTER, e. Mud. It is considered lucky to bring mud into the house in January.

JAUNCE, e. A weary journey.

"I döänt justly know how far it is to Hellingly, but you'll have a middlin' jaunce before you get there."

JAWLED-OUT, w. Excessively fatigued.

JIB, e. The under-lip. To hang the jib, is to look cross.

JIGGER-PUMP, e. A pump used in breweries to force the beer into the vats.

JOHNNY, m. or LORD JOHN, e.

"Old Johnny" is one of the numerous names given to the ague. Another is Axey.

"Old Johnny has been running his finger down my back."

A spider is considered a useful insect for the cure of the ague. If taken internally, it should be rolled up in a cobweb and swallowed like a pill. If applied externally, it should be placed in a nutshell and hung round the neck in a bag of black silk. The ague generally hangs about Sussex people a long time.

JOINT-STEDDLE, or JOINT-STOOL, w. A stool framed by joinery work, so called in distinction from stools rudely formed of a single block.

"Away with the joint-stools, remove the court-cupboard." – Romeo and Juliet, Act i. sc. 5.

JORAM, m. A capacious bowl or goblet; called in Norfolk a Jeroboam.

Brede Place

JOSSING-BLOCK, e. or JOSS BLOCK; also called upping stone, mounting stone or horse block. A block by which a rider mounts his horse, often seen at the gate of a country churchyard in Sussex.

JOSS-UP, e. To mount a horse.
"Ah! she josses up like a feather, she döánt want no jossing-block nor chair either."

JOSTLE, m. To cheat.

JOUND, m. Joined.
"I jound in with them up at Burwash Wheel, and they jostled me out of ninepence."

JOURNEY, m. [Journée, French.] A day's work. This word is spelt in old parochial account-books jorney, but in such MSS. the spelling seems to have depended upon the task or caprice of the writer.

JOY. A jay.
"Poor old Master Crockham, he's in terrible order, surelye! The meece have taken his peas, and the joys have got at his beans, and the snags have spilt all his lettuce."

JUB, e. To move slowly and heavily, like a sluggish horse.

JUB, e. A slow trot.

JUG. A nickname given to the men of Brighton.

JUMPING-BETTY, e. or JUMPING-JACK. Impatiens balsamina. Specifically Noli-me-tangere; Touch-me-not.

JUMP-RO UND-AND-HANG-BY-NOTHING, e. To make haste.
She's a capital good girl to work, she can jump round and hang by nothing, I can tell you."

JUMP-UP-AND-KISS-ME, m. The pansy. Viola tricolor.

Also called Kiss-me; Kiss-me-at-the-garden-gate; and Three faces-under-a-hood.

JUNE-BUG, m. The green beetle, or the Rose beetle. Also the cock-chafer.

JUSTABOUT, m. Certainly; extremely.

"I justabout did enjoy myself up at the Cristial Palace on the Foresters' day, but there was a terr'ble gurt crowd; I should think there must have been two or three hundred people a-scrouging about."

JUST-BEAST, or JOIST-BEAST, e.

A beast taken in to graze. This word is probably a corruption of agist beast. Agistment was the feeding of cattle in a common pasture at a fixed price. In the year 1531 the agistment of a horse for the summer cost 3s. 4d.

JUSTLY, m. Exactly. Rightly.

"I döänt justly know how old I be, but I knows I be above sixty years of age; for ye see I went to work when I was somewhere's about nine years old (that was in old Mus Ridge's time) and I kep on till I was some wheres about fower-and-twenty; and then a young woman got me into trouble, and I was forced to goo away to sea; but I didn't hold to that above six or seven years, and then I come home and got drawed for the Militia and sarved ten year, and then volunteered for a sodger and sarved by time fifteen years; and then I comed back to the farm, and there I've worked for fower-and-farty year, till I got quite entirely eat up with the rheumattics, and now I aint done naun for these last ten years, and sometimes they be better than what they be other-some; so I knows I be above sixty year old, though I döänt justly know how old I be."

The account works out that he was 100.

81

K

KEBLOCK. w. The wild turnip.

KEDDLE-NETS. Stake nets.

KEELER, m. [Coélan, Ang. Sax., to cool.] A shallow tub used for cooling beer.

KELL, m. or KILL, w. [Cyl, Welsh.] A kiln.

"I've been quite out of kelter ever sen I've lived up aside of the lime kells; the reek's enough to choke one otherwhiles."

KELLICK, m. A romp.

KELTER, m, or KILTER, w. Condition.

"This farm seems in very good kelter."

KEN, m. [Corruption of Kin.]

KERF, w. [Ang. Sax., ceorfan, to cut; cyrf, a cutting.] The cut made by a saw; a notch. Also a long horizontal cut made partway through a board for the purpose of bending it.

KETTLE, w. A swelling; a dark lump found in suet or pork.

KETTLY, w. Full of kettles or kernels.

KEVELING, m. The name given at Brighton to the skate; at Hastings the fish is called "a maid", and at Dover "a damsel."

KEX, e. The dry hollow stalk of hogweed, cow parsley, and other unbelliferæ.

KICKEL, e. [Cicel, Ang. Sax.] A sort of flat cake, with sugar and currants strewn on the top.

KID, e. A small wooden tub.

KID, w. The pod of peas or beans.

Stopham Bridge

KIDDLE, e. To entice; to coax.

KIDDLE, e., or KITTLE. [Citelian, Ang. Sax., to tickle.] To tickle.
"Those thunderbugs did kiddle so that I couldn't keep still no hows."

KIDDLE, w. Delicate.

KILK, m., or KELK. Charlock, sinapis arvensis, a weed with a yellow flower which grows among the corn.
The employment of children at kilk-pulling is a serious obstacle to education in the agricultural districts.

KIME, m., or KINE. A weazel. Also called Futtice.
A lady who had been giving a lesson to a Sunday school class upon Pharoah's dreams, was startled to find that all the boys supposed that the fat and lean kine were weazels.

KIMMEL, m., or KYMELL. A tub used for salting meat, and in the brewhouse.

KIND, m. Fat; doing well, said of beasts.

KINK, m. [Kink, Dutch, a twist in a rope.] To twist, entangle.

KISSING-GATE, w. The same as a cuckoo-gate. Also called To she-and-fro-she-gate.

KISS-ME, e. The wild heartsease. Viola tricolor. Pansy.
Also called: Jump-up-and-kiss me, Kiss-me-at-the-garden-gate and Three-faces-under-a-hood.

KIVER. m. A large shallow tub.

KNAP. [Cnæp, Ang. Sax., top.] The top of a hill, or any piece of rising ground.

KNETTAR, e.; or KNITTLE, w. [Cnittan, Ang. Sax., to knit.] A string fastened to the mouth of a sack to tie it with.

KNOW, m. Used as a substantive for knowledge. (Slang ' in the know.')
"Poor fellow, he has got no know whatsumdever, but his sister's a nice knowledgeable girl."

KNOWLEDGEABLE, e. Well-educated.

KNUCKER. [Hnægan, Ang. Sax.] To neigh or whinny.

L

LADDER-TYING. Fastening the upper branches of the hop-plant to the pole, which is reached by women standing on ladders.

LADES. [Ladan, Ang. Sax., to load.] Rails which project round the top of a waggon to enable it to bear a greater load. Sometimes called Ladders.

LADSLOVE. Southernwood Artemesia abrotanum.

LADYCOW. The ladybird. Other names are:– Bishop Barnaby, Fly Golding and God Almighty's Cow. It is held extremely unlucky to kill a cricket, a ladybird, a swallow, martin, robin redbreast, or wren. Or a spider or red spider.

LADY'S-SMOCK. Convolvulus sepium. The (greater) bindweed of the hedges. Also called Milkmaids and Old-man's nightcap.

The name Ladysmock is more often given to Cardamine pratensis, which is also called Cuckoo flower or Milk-maid.

LAG, or LEG, w. and m. A long narrow marshy meadow, usually by the side of a stream.

LAINES. Open tracts of arable land at the foot of the Downs.

LAMBSTONGUE. Plantago media. Hoary Plantain.

LAMENTABLE, m. Very.
This word seems to admit of three degrees of comparison, which are indicated by the accentuation, thus,–
Positive – Lamentable, as usually pronounced
Comparative – Larmentable.
Superlative – Larmentaable.

Hangleton House

"Master Chucks he says to me says he, ' 'tis larmentable purty weather, Master Crockham.' 'Larmentable!' says I."

LAND, m. Low ground, especially arable land, as distinguished from the hill used in the Southdown country.

LANSCOT, or LANDSCOTE. The assessment of lands for the maintenance of the church now obsolete.

LAPSY. Lazy, slow, indifferent.

LARDER A gamekeeper's larder is the place where he nails up the weazels, stoats and vermin which he kills.

LARDER, m. (Corruption of Ladder.) Like arder for adder.

"Master's got a lodge down on the land yonder, and as I was going across totherday-morning to fetch a larder we keeps there, a lawyer catched holt 'an me and scratched my face."

LASH, m. To get into a passion.

"He makes me lash and swear otherwhile when he be so lapsy; soonasever I'm backturned he's off after the birds-nestes, or up to some game or another."

LAST, e. A last of herrings is ten thousand.

LAST, e. A court of twenty-four jurats who levy rates for keeping up the marshes. That is for the Romney and Guldeford Marshes. For Pevensey they were twelve in number, called Shawers.

LASUS. A water meadow.

LATS. [Latta. Ang. Sax.] Laths.

LARTIN, w., or LATTEN. Plate tin. Spelt lattyn in an inventory dated 1549, but in that year people spelt

as they pleased.

LAURENCE. A mysterious individual whose influence is supposed to produce indolence. "Old Laurence has got hold of me" means "I have got a fit of idleness."

LAVANT, w. [Lafian, Ang. Sax., to sprinkle with water; or, Laver, French, to wash.] A violent flow of water. "How it did rain! It ran down the street in a lavant."

LAWYER, e. A long bramble full of thorns, so called because, "When once they gets a holt an ye, ye döánt easy get shut of 'em."
Used by boys to extract rabbits from their buries, engaging their fur by twisting. Also called Follower.

LAY, m., or LEY. [Leag, Ang. Sax.] Land laid down for pasture; not permanently, but to be broken up every three of four years. (Cf; Ley.)

LAYLOCK, m. The lilac tree.

LAY-UP, m. To hide and lie in wait for any one.

LEAKWAY.t A road dividing one furlong from another in the tenantry acre.

LEAN, m. Unprofitable.
"Ah, sir! stone-breaking's a lean job for those that aint used to it."

LEAN-TO, m. A shed constructed against the side of another building.

LEAP, e. [Leap, Ang. Sax., a basket; also a basket for catching fish.] A large deep basket.

LEAP, e. Half-a-bushel.

LEAR. Thin; hungry; faint. Especially for want of food.
"I shall be glad when we gets home, I feel a bit leary."

LEARN. To teach. Usually said "Larn."

"I'll lay-up for him one of these nights and leather him middlin' if I catches him; I'll learn him how to steal my apples, letbehow'twill."

LEASE, m. [Lese, Ang. Sax., gathering, from lesan, to gather.] To glean.

LEASE-WHEAT, m. The ears of corn picked up by the gleaners.

LEAST. [Læstan,Ang.Sax.] To last. "I've picked up a little leasewheat, but that wont least very long; leastways not above a week or two."

LEASTWAYS. [Leastwise]. At least.

LEATHER. To flog. Usually said "Lather."

LEAZE, m. [Læse, Ang. Sax., of pasturage, of common; i.e. common right of pasturage.] The right of feed for a bullock or sheep on a common.

LEETLE. [Diminutive of Little.]

"I never see one of these here gurt men there's s'much talk about in the peapers, only once, and that was up at Smiffle Show adunnamanyyears agoo. Prime minister, they told me he was, up at Lunnon; a leetle, lear, miserable, skinny-looking chap as ever I see. 'Why,' I says, 'we döänt count our minister to be much, but he's a deal primer-looking than what yourn be'."

LENT. A loan.

"I thank you for the lent of your horse."

LETBEHOW'TWILI, m. An expression always pronounced as one word, meaning, let the consequences be what they may; abbreviated in West Sussex into behowtel.

LEW. [Hleowth, Ang. Sax., warmth.] Sheltered from the wind "My garden is nice and lew."

LEWTH. Shelter.

"You wont find but very little lewth on the hill."

LIBBET, e. A stick used to knock down fruit from the trees. When throwing at cocks was a fashionable sport, the stick which was thrown had lead let in at the end, and was called a libbet.

"The old custom of throwing at cocks on Shrove Tuesday is said to date from the fact of the crowing of a cock having prevented our Saxon ancestors from massacreing their conquerors, another part of our ancestors, the Danes, on the morning of a Shrove Tuesday, when they were asleep in their beds."

– Brand's Popular Antiquities.

LIDDS. m. Large open fields.

LIGHTING. For lightning.

"There was a good deal of lighting last night."

LIKE. This word added to adjectives somewhat qualifies the force of their meaning.

"She seems so melancholy-like" means "she seems rather melancholy."

LILY, m.† The field convolvulus. Convolvulus arvensis. Also called Devil weed.

LINK. [Hlinc, Ang. Sax., a ridge of land.] A word used in the South downs for a green wooded bank, always on the side of a hill between two pieces of cultivated land.

LIONS MOUTH, m. Ground Ivy. Glecoma hederacea. Also (among other names) Alehoof and Gill ale, because used in brewing ale. The leaves are often dried and made into tea, called Gill-tea

LIP. A wooden box of a peculiar shape, which is carried by the seedsman when sowing. Curved to fit the body: the same as seed-cord or seed-lip.

LIPPY, m. Impertinent; apt to answer saucily.

LIST, m. To leak.

"That new lean-to of yourn is a poor temporary thing; I reckon it wont least long, for the water lists through the roof already."

LITHER, e. Idle.

LITHER. (Lithe, from lithe, Ang. Sax., gentle; soft.) Supple; lithy; pliable.

LITTEN. [Lictun, Sax.] A church yard.

LITTER, m. Loose straw or any-

The Ypres Tower, Rye

thing thrown into a farmyard for cattle to lie upon and tread into manure.

LIVE; e. Real.

"She thinks she looks like a lady, but no one would take her for a live lady."

LIVERSICK. A hangnail on the finger.

LIZENED. Lean; shrunk, as applied to corn

LOANST. A loan.

"Will you lend mother the loanst of a little tea."

LOCH.* The rut of a cart-wheel.

LODE.* [Lád, Ang. Sax., a way; a canal.] A drift-way, or cut for water; a ford.

LODGE, m. An outhouse; a shed. Particularly, a shed having one or more sides open. E.g., Cart-Cow-lodge.

"I found him here as melancholy as a lodge in a warren." – Much Ado About Nothing, Act ii. sc. 1.

LODGE. [Logian, Ang. Sax.] To alight or fall on anything so as to remain there.

"My ball has lodged up on the window-sill."

LODGED. Corn or grass beaten down by wind and rain is said to be lodged.

"We'll make foul weather with
    despised tears;
Our sighs, and they, shall lodge the
    summer corn,
And make a dearth in this revolting
    land" – Richard II. Act iii. sc. 3.

LONESOME. Lonely; far from neighbours.

LONG-DOG, m. A greyhound. A Grew.

LONG-PURPLES. The flowers of orchis mascula. Early purple orchis: leaves stained with dark purple spots.

"And long purples
That liberal shepherds give a grosser name." – Hamlet. Act iv. sc. 7.

LOOKER, e. [Lócian, Ang. Sax., to look.] A shepherd or herdsman; a man employed to look after cattle in the marshes.

LOOK-OUT, e. To open. Said of a window.

"It's no manner of use your trying; the window wont look out, for there was such a terr'ble big draught come in that father he took and made it fast."

LOPE-OFF. To go away in a secret, sly manner (probably connected with the word elope). (The same root: hleóp, Ang. Sax., leapt, ran, fled.)

"The old dog was round here just now, but he must have loped off somewhere, he's gone off along with the shepherd very like."

LORDINGS, e. The best kind of faggots. The branches and tops taken off the wood which is being cut for hop-poles.

LOURDY.* [Lourd; French, dull.] Heavy; sluggish.

LURRY, e. A rapid, indistinct mode of reading.

LURRY, e. To hurry over work in a careless, slovenly manner.

LUSTY, m. Fat; in good order.

"You look as though what you've had sen' you was here last has done you good, you be got quite lusty!"

LUTON. A projection from a house, such as a bow window.

M

MAD. Enraged.

"Ah! he just will be mad if he comes to hear an't."

MAID, e. This word is still sometimes used for children of both sexes who are too young to work.

"Words not a few were once applied to both sexes alike which are now restricted to the female, it is so even with girl, which once meant a young person of either sex." – Archbishop Trench, English Past and English Present.

MAKE or MEND, e. To interfere.

"He must go his own way, I'm not a-going to make or mend any more."

MALT-STIRRER, w. A stick with a sort of lattice-work at the end, used for stirring the malt in brewing.

MANNERED, m. A meadow abounding in sweet grasses is said to be good mannered.

"You wunt have such a very out-de-way gurt swarth, but 'tis countable purty mannered stuff, I call it."

MARCHET, w. "Every widow holding by her bench is bound by the custom of the manor to pay unto the lord of the said manor, at the time of her next marriage after she is first a widow, her best beast of any manner of quick cattle, for and in the name of a Marchant, otherwise called a Marchet." – Customs of the Manor of Bosham.

MARE, w. A shallow lake. Broad mare Common: Maresfield.

Mere and mare are regular Sussex developments of Old English Meer. – Mawer & Stenton, Place Names of Sussex.

MARESTAILS. Streaky white clouds, said to indicate wind.

MARTIN, e. When a cow has two calves, one of which is a male and the other a female, the latter is called a free-martin, and it is supposed that she will always be barren.

MARVEL. Hoarhound. (Should be horehound.) Ballota nigra.

MASK. Completely covered with anything, but generally mud or blood

"Why! you're one mask! Where ever have you been?" "The boys shoved me into the masoner's mortar mixen."

MASONER. m. A bricklayer.

MASTER. (Pronounced Mars, Mas or Mass.) (Marce is really nearer the sound round which the word said varies.) The distinctive title of a married labourer.

A single man will be called by his (Christian name all his life long; but a married man, young or old, is "Master" even to his most intimate friend and fellow workmen, as long as he can earn his own livelihood; but as soon as he becomes past work he turns into "the old gentleman," leaving the bread-winner to rank as master of the household

"Master" is quite a distinct title from "Mr.," which is always pronounced Mus, thus, –

Mus Smith is the employer.

Master Smith is the man he employs.

MASTER. The old custom of the wife speaking of her husband as

Chichester Cathedral

her "master" still lingers among elderly people; but both the word and the reasonableness of its use are rapidly disappearing in the present generation.

It may be mentioned here that they say in Sussex that the rosemary will never blossom except where "the mistus" is master. 'Tis said too that catmint will not grow in one's garden unless it be stolen.

MASTERFUL. Overbearing. Self-willed.

MAUND. [Mand, Ang. Sax., a

90

basket.] A hand basket with two handles.

MAUNDER, e. [Maudire, French, to curse.] To mutter or grumble. To speak with a beggar's whine; also a beggar who carries a maund.

MAUNDER. To wander about thoughtfully.

MAVIN.* The margin.

MAWKIN, w. A scarecrow.

MAXON, m. [Meox, Ang. Sax., dung.] A manureheap.

MAYBE and MAYHAP. Perhaps.
"May be you knows Mass Pilbeam? No! döänt ye? Well, he was a very sing'lar marn was Mass Pilbeam, a very sing'lar marn! He says to he's mistus one day, he says, 'tis a long time, says he, sence I've took a holiday – so cardenly, nex marnin' he laid abed till purty nigh seven o'clock, and then he brackfustes, and then he goos down to the shop and buys fower ounces of barca, and he sets hisself down on the maxon, and there he set, and there he smoked and smoked and smoked all the whole day long, for, says he, 'tis a long time sence I've had a holiday! Ah, he was a very sing'lar marn – a very sing'lar marn indeed."

MAYBUG, m. Cockchafer. Also called June-bug.

MAYWEED, m. Anthemis cotula. Morgan. Stinking Camomile.

MEAD. [Maéd, Ang. Sax.] Still used for meadow.

MEAL. [Maél, Ang. Sax., a fixed portion.] The quantity of milk taken from the cow at one milking.

MEECE, m. Mice.
"The meece just have tarrified my peas."

Among other Sussex remedies it is said that a mouse roasted alive is good for the whooping-cough. Whether it is really good for the whooping cough or not I cannot say, but I am sure it must be bad for the mouse.

MEND, m. To spread out manure (amendment) over a field.

MERESMAN, m. (Meáre, Ang. Sax., a boundary.) A parish officer who attends to the roads, bridges and water-courses.

MERRY-TREE, w.∞ (Merise, French.) The wild cherry tree. Cérasus syluestris.

MERSC. [Mersc., Ang. Sax.] A marsh.

MESH, m. (Marsh). The Southdown folk always speak of Pevensey level as the Mesh.
"I went down to Pemsey last week, and walked out on the Mesh. Beautiful place, surelye! No hills, no trees, nor nothing to interrupt the view."

MESSENGERS. Large white flying clouds, indicating rough weather.

MEUSE, w. A hole through a hedge made by a rabbit or hare; an old French sporting term.

MEW. [Méu, Ang. Sax.] A seagull.

MIDDLING. This word has many different meanings which are expressed by the tone of voice in which it is said.
It may mean very much, as "He lashed out middlin', I can tell ye!" Or it may mean tolerably well, as "I döänt know but what she made out purty middlin'."
Or it may mean very bad, as, "How did the wedding go off?" "Middling, thank you, sir." "What,

only middling! wasn't it all right?" "Why, no sir, not quite, for you see the parson he entirely forgot all about it, and he'd gone away, so we was forced to wait in church two hours."

MIDGE. [Mycg, Ang. Sax., a gnat.] All gnats are called midges in Sussex.

MIFF. To give slight offence; to displease.

MILEMAS, m. [Corruption of Michælmas.]

MILE-STONES. The churches in the Downs are called Sussex mile-stones.

MILKMAIDS, e. The flowers of the convolvulus sepium. The great bindweed. Also called Lady's smocks and Old-man's-nightcap.

MILK-MAIDS, w.† Birds-foot trefoil. Lotus corniculatus. Also called Butter-and-eggs.

MIND, m. [Mynan, Ang. Sax.] To remember.

"I minds him well, he was along here last Milemas."

MINNIS, e. A piece of rising ground.

One of the rocks on the East Hill, at Hastings, is called the Minnis Rock. In Kent the word is used for a high common.

MINTS. The mites in cheese, meal or flour.

MINTY. Full of mites.

MISAGIFT.* or MISAGAFT. Misgiven; mistaken.

MISACREE, m. To disagree.

"I döánt see how anyone can be

Piddinghoe

off from misagreeing with these here people next door, for the old man's that miserable that he wont lend nothing to nobody, and the children be that mischieful that one döánt know where to be for 'em."

MISCHIEFUL, m. or MISCHEEVIOUS. Full of mischief.

MISERABLE, m. Miserly; stingy.

MISHEROON. [Mousseron, French.] A mushroom. Or Musheroon.

MISLIKE. [Mislícian, Ang. Sax.] To dislike.

"My lord of Winchester, I know your mind;
'Tis not my speeches that you do mis like,
But 'tis my presence that doth trouble you." – 11 Henry VI, Act i. sc. l.

MISS. Abbreviation of mistress. The title of a married woman; single ladies being addressed as Mrs.

MISSUS. Is the usual pronunciation of mistress.

It is very difficult to say at what age a Sussex man's wife ceases to be his mistus and becomes the old 'ooman, and finally lapses (probably in her second childhood) into the old gal.

MISWORD, m. A cross, angry, or abusive word.

"I am sure my master's never given me a misword all the years we've been married."

MIXEN. [Mixen, Ang. Sax., from mix, meox, dung.] A heap of mixed manure. A dunghill.

MIZMAZE. Confusion.

"He came upon me so quick, and axed me so suddent, I was all of a mizmaze."

MOAK. [Max, masc, Ang. Sax., a mesh, a noose.] The mesh of a net.

"Ordered, that no fisherman of the town should fish with any trawl net whereof the moak holdeth not five inches size throughout."   –   Hastings Corporation Records, 1604.

MOCK-BEGGAR-HALL. A house which has an inviting external aspect, but within is poor and bare, dirty and disappointing. A farm near Rye bears this name.

MOLE PLOUGH, w. A draining plough.

MOMMICK, m., or MAMMICK. To cut or carve awkwardly or unevenly.

"Whether his fall enraged him, or how 'twas, he did so set his teeth and tear it; O, I warrant how he mammockcd it." – Coriolanus, Act i. sc. 3.

MONEY-PURSE. A purse.

MONGER. [Mangere, Ang. Sax., a dealer.] A man who has anything for sale.

A field at Selmston is called The Monger's Plot.

MOONSHINE. Smuggled spirits.

MOONSHINER. A beast that will not fat; a diseased beast that has to be driven off to the butcher's yard by night.

MORE. As big-more, or as long-more, means as big again, or as long again.

" 'Tis as fur more from here to Hellingly as what it is from here to Hailsham."

MORGAN. May-weed. Anthemis cotula. Stinking camomile. Also said Mauven.

MORT. [Icel.; Mart, neuter of margr, many.] A great many.

Blackdown

"Yes, I've got a mort of children, but there's not one that's bringing in anything."

MORTACIOUS. Mortal; very.

"My old sow's mortacious bad, surelye!"

MORTAL. A term of reproach.

"What a young mortal that he's always at something!"

MOSS-IN-GINRAL, m. Generally.

"I most-in-ginral goos to church, but I goos to chapel otherwhile when 'tis so slubby."

MOTHER, e. To take care of.

"I döánt mind mothering the dog for you for a week or two."

MOTHERING. The service for the churching of women.

It is considered most unlucky for a woman after giving birth to a child to cross the high-road, or to pay a visit before she has been to

94

church to return thanks.

Lupton, in his first book of notable things, ed. 1660, p. 49, says:– "If a man be the first that a woman meets after she comes out of the Church, when she is newly churched, it signifies that her next child will be a boy; if she meets a woman, then a wench is likely to be her next child. This is credibly reported to me to be true."

MOTHERING-PEW. The pew reserved for women who desire to be churched It is on record that an elderly maiden-lady once found her way by accident into the mothering-pew in a strange church, and joined devoutly in the service, which included that appointed for the churching of women, but did not discover that she had her self been churched till the clerk handed her the alms-dish for her offering.

MOTHER-WO. A contraction of "come hither wilt thou."

A carter's call to his horse to come towards him.

MOTHERY. Mouldy; generally applied to liquor which has become thick and incrusted.

MOWBURNED, m. Hay which has fermented in the stack. Or in the mow.

MOX.† [Ang. Sax., max; Dutch,

masche.l The mesh of a net. (Called at Hastings a moak.)

MUCK, m. To hurry; to overwork.

"She's mucking about from morning to night."

MUCKED-UP. All in confusion.

"I döánt know as you'll find a seat, for we be all so mucked-up this morning."

MUCK-GRUBBER. A sordid miser. The sort of man who would search in the dung-heap or any filthy place for the sake of money.

MUCK-OUT. To clean thoroughly. Especially to clean out a stall.

"I döánt think that old house has been properly mucked out for the last ten years."

MUDDLE-ABOUT. To do a little work.

"I'm ever so much better, and I shouldn't wonder but what I shall be able to muddle about in a day or two."

MUDGELLY.* Broken, as straw is by being trodden by cattle.

MUSH, e. A marsh. Also Mersc and Mesh.

"He's a stupid mumchance chap; seems as though he'd lived all his time down in the mush and never spoken to no-one."

MUSIC. Any musical instrument.

N

NABBLE, m. To chatter; to gossip; to idle about.

NABBLER. A gossip.

NAIL. A weight of eight pounds.

NAPERY, w. [Nappe, French, a table-cloth.] Linen, but especially table linen.

NARRE, w. [Knorren, Dutch, to growl.] To growl like a dog.

NATIVE. Birthplace, native place. Used as a substantive.

"Heathfield is my native. I was borned at the cottage just beyond the pay-gate where there's postes beside the road."

NAUGHTY-MAN'S-PLAYTHING. Stinging nettle. Urtica dioica.

NAUN, m. Nothing.

NAUN-BUT. Only; answering to the northern expression nobbut.

"I should have gone to Lewes market naunbut I hadn't got naun to take there."

NEAR, m. Stingy. Close; close-fisted.

"I only ask 'im for a shillun' but he's that near he wouldn't give me naun." – At a charity bazaar.

Bayham Abbey

NEAT. Exact; full; said of measurements, as " 'Tis ten rod neat, no more nor no less."

NEB, e. [Neb, Ang. Sax., the bill or beak.] The pole of an ox-cart, or timber tug, so called from its shape.

NEB, m. The handle of a scythe. The short handle, called also nib, dole, or handpin. The long handle is called a snethe or snead.

NEIGHBOUR'S FARE, e. The same bad luck.

"We've got neighbour's fare, for we've neither of us got an umbrella."

NEIGHBOUR-TOGETHER. To be good friends.

NESTLE. To be restless.

NESTLE-ABOUT, m. To work about a little in and out of the house.

"I aint done naun but just nestle about house for the last three weeks, and I be quite nett-up this weather."

NETTLE-SPRING. The nettle-rash.

NETT-UP. Exhausted with cold. Like field-fares in hard frost.

NEWS. To tell anything as news. "It was newsed about."

NEXDY. [Contraction of next day.] The day after to-morrow.

NI, w., NIDE, or NYE. [Nid, French, a nest; spelt ni in old French.] A brood of pheasants.

NIDGET, e. A little bug.

NIDGET. A horse-hoe used for cleaning the ground between rows of hops, called in some parts of East Sussex an idget.

NIFF. To quarrel: to be offended.

NIP; e. A stingy fellow; a close and sharp bargainer; just honest and no more.

NIPPER, m. A common nickname for the youngest member of the family, or for one who is unusually small for his age.

NOD. The back of the neck. "It catched me right across the nod of my neck."

NOGGING. Courses of bricks worked in between a frame of wood work in a building.

NOHOWS, m. In no way. Often expanded into "no-hows-de-wurreld," for no how in the world.

NONCE, w. Purpose; intent; design.

"I have cases of buckram for the nonce, to immask our noted outward garments." – I Henry IV, Act i. sc. 2.

NON-PLUSH.   [Non-plus.] Completely bewildered.

NO-ONE-WHERES. Superlative form of nowhere.

"I shouldn't have been no ways consarned about it, naunbut my mistus she took on so; she was quite non-plushed she was, for she couldn't find that young nipper no-one-wheres."

NO-OUGHT, m. "You had no-ought" is the same as "you ought not." Or rather "you had no right." "You had no-ought to interfere with the nipper."

NORATE, m. [Corruption of Orate; as nidget, from idget.] With a snatching at 'Narrate.' To talk officiously and fussily about other people's business.

"Master Norman he got nabbling over it, so it very soon got norated about all down the street."

NORATION. An unnecessary

publication of any piece of news or a secret.

"You have no-ought to have made such a noration about nothing, for you warn't no-ways consarned."

NOWARD.§ (Possibly of Norwegian, or reputedly Norwegian pattern). A peculiar kind of net.

NOSE-HOLES. Nostrils. Nostril really means nosehole (from Ang. Sax. nósthyrl: O.E. nosethril or nosethirl. Thyrl or thyrel meaning a hole.)

NOT, w. [Hnot, Ang. Sax., shorn, cut.] Polled; said of sheep or cows without horns.

"Mus' Stapley he's been and bought some more of these here not cows. I can't fancy them things no hows-de-wurreld."

NOTCH. A run at cricket; so called from the custom in the country districts of reckoning the runs by notches cut in a stick.

NOTTABLE, m. [Notable, French, remarkable.] Thrifty; industrious; and clever in housewifery.

Mr. Lower says that this word is never applied in Sussex to a man.

"Mrs. Allbones she be a nottable 'ooman, surelye!"

NOVER, e. High land above a precipitous bank.

NOW-AND-AGAIN. Sometimes.

"I goos across the nover now-and-agin, but I mostly keeps to the road, for 'tis terrble nubbly for walking."

NO-WAYS. In no way.

NUBBLY, e. In lumps; full of small clods.

NUNTING, e. Awkward looking.

NUNTY, e. Dressed in a shabby or old-fashioned way.

NUNTY, m. Sulky.

"Ye be middlin' nunty this marnin' seemingly; I döánt know naun what's putt ye out."

NURT, w. To nurture; to train or bring up a child.

NURT, m. To entice; to allure.

"He got linked-in with some chaps as wasn't no good, and they nurted him away, and he never come back nuther."

NUTHER. [Corruption of Neither.]

O

OAST-HAIR. A hair sieve used in oast-houses.

OAST-HOUSE. A place for drying hops.

With respect to the origin of this word, Mr. Durrant Cooper gives the following explanation,–

"As hops were introduced into England from Flanders, probably persons who understood the culture and cure of the article were brought with them; hence the word heuse, a house, was applied by these foreigners to the building where the hops were dried; subsequently heuse was corrupted into haust or oast, and the word house very improperly appended by those who did not know the import of the original"

I think, however, that Rev. J. C. Egerton, of Burwash, has got nearer to the true derivation of the word He informs me that, in Dutch, August is called oogst-maand, the harvest month, and tracing a connection between oogst and oast, he is of opinion that oast house is nothing more than oost-haus, the harvest-house, and that a close similitude may be found in the words August, août, oogst, and oast.

With respect to this suggestion, Rev. W. W. Skeat considers that oogst is more likely to be connected with the Latin, Augustus, and that the meaning of harvest is quite secondary. He is of opinion that oost in oast-house is a mere corruption or dialectic variation of the Dutch eest, a drying kiln.

OBEDIENCE. [Obeisance.] A bow or curtsey.

OCKLANDS, m. Hocklands.

OILS, w. The beards of barley.

OLD CLEM. A figure dressed up with a wig and beard and pipe, and set up over the door of the inn where the blacksmiths held their feast in honour of their patron Saint on St. Clement's day (23rd November).

OLD-FATHER, m. The person who gives away the bride at her wedding.

Among the labouring classes in Sussex it is not the custom for the bride to be accompanied to church by her father. The bridal procession is very simple, and consists usually of four persons only – the bride and bridegroom, the bridesmaid, and the old father, who is usually the sweetheart of the bridesmaid if she is a single woman (which is not necessarily the case.)

I was once marrying a shepherd who had arrayed himself in a very tight pair of white kid gloves; and suggested before the service began that he had better remove the glove from his right hand. "What!" he exclaimed, "Must I have her off? Then if she takes as long to come off as she did to putt on, we shan't get this here job over to day."

OLD-MAN'S-NIGHTCAP. Convolvulus sepium. The great bindweed. Also called Lady's-smock, and Milkmaids.

ONE, e. To be at one, is to be consistent and determined.

ONE. To be one, is to be good friends; to be at two is to quarrel.

Amberley Castle. Entrance to the churchyard

OOD, m. [Corruption of Wood.] Like 'ooman for woman.

OPEN. m. Not spayed: said of a sow.

ORATION. A fuss, not necessarily expressed by words.
   "He makes such an oration about anything."

ORDER, m. Bad temper.
   "He's in middlin' order, I can tell ye."

ORE, e. Seaweeds washed on shore by the tides.

ORNARY. [Corruption of Ordinary.] (Or rather, an elision of extraordinary. Inferior: unwell.

ORTS, m. Odds and ends; fragments of broken victuals.

"The fractions of her faith, orts of her
    love,
The fragments, scraps, the bits, and
    greasy reliques,
Of her o'er eaten faith, are bound to
    Diomed."
– Troilus and Cressida, Act v, sc. 2.

OTHERSOME. Some other.

"Sometimes my old gal's better than what she be othersome, but she be hem ornary again to-dee."

OTHERWHERES. Some other place.
"The King hath sent me otherwhere."
– King Henry VIII, Act ii. sc. 2.

OTHERWHILE, or OTHER-WHILES. Sometimes; occasionally. Now and then.

"I has a horn of beer otherwhile, but never nothing to do me no hurt."

"I jest goos an' has a look roun' otherwhiles."

OUGHT, m. See No-ought.

OURN. Ours. (Cf. Hisn.)

OUT-ASKED, or OUT-OF-ASK. To have had the banns published three times.

OUT-BOUNDERS, w. A word used in old parochial account books for ratepayers who pay rates in a parish where they do not reside.

OUT-DE-WAY, m. [Corruption of out of the way.]

"I never did see such tedious out-de-way larmentable poor ground in all my borns."

OUT-STAND. To stand out against; to oppose and overcome.

Beachy Head

"He wanted to have the calf for three pound ten, but I out-stood him upon that, for all that he was so set and contrairy."

OVEN-RAKE, e. [Ófenraca, Ang. Sax.] A rake for clearing the ashes aside in a brick oven.

OVEN-SLICE, w. An iron shovel for taking the ashes out of the oven.

OVER, e. To cross over.

"You must over the bridge and keep straight on a-head."

OVERGET, e. To overtake.

OWLET. m. A moth.

OX-STEDDLE m. Stabling or stalls for oxen.

Oxen are still used as draught beasts; the Sussex breed being specially useful for the purpose. A team of eight oxen drawing a load is not an unusual sight in East Sussex, though it is not seen so frequently as it was twenty years ago.

Now the roads are better they frequently don't shoe the oxen as they always used to do.

OX-TIGHTS, w. Chains for use with oxen.

P

PACKLED, m. Speckled.

PADDLE, m. To trample about in the wet and dirt

PAINFUL. Painstaking.

There is an inscription on a brass in Selmeston Church, dated 1639, which commences thus,–
The body of Henry Rogers,
A painfull preacher in this church
Two and thirty yeeres.

PAIR-OF-BARS, w. Rails made to lift out of the sockets, so as to admit of a cart passing through; called in East and Mid Sussex a bar-way.

PALLANT. [Palent, Palant, Ang. Sax., a palace.] The Pallant is a district of Chichester opening from the West-street.

Murray says "It forms a miniature Chichester with its own four streets, and is the palatinate, or Archbishop's peculiar."

PALM. The bloom of the willow, which is worn on Palm Sunday. Also called from its colour and quality "Goslings."

In Kent yew-trees are always called palms.

PANDLE, m. A shrimp. Also used in Kent

PANNAGE, m. The mast of the oak and beech on which swine feed in the woods.

A copyhold right to these existed in one of the manors of Brighton.

PARGET. [Old English pariet, a wall; derived from the Latin paies.]

To plaster with cement; especially to plaster the inside of a chim-ney with cement made of cow-dung and lime.

Parget has a soft 'g'. The word is not now local.

PARLY, or PARLEY FRANCY. [Parler, French, to talk.] To talk French, or to talk unintelligibly.

A fisherman said, "I can make shift to parly a bit myself, but deuce-a-bit can I make out when the Frenchies begins to parly me."

A maid servant being asked who was with her master, answered that she didn't rightly know, but she knew he was a Parly-German !

PARSON-ROOK or PASSON-ROOK. A Royston-crow. The hoodie- or grey-crow.

This species has obtained the specific name given by the Romans to some bird of the crow kind, deemed of unlucky omen – sinistra cornix. (Or Coruus Cornix Cornix.)

PARTIAL. To be partial to anything, means, to like it, generally in the sense of relishing.

"I be very partial to a few pandles."

PARTICULAR, m. To look particular, is to look unwell.

"He's been looking very particular for some time past."

PASSEL, m. [Corruption of Parcel.] Used for flock: a passel of boys; a passel of nonsense.

PASSTIME, m. Time passed.

"He mustn't expect to get well all in a minute. I tell him there's no passtime for that yet."

PASTIME, m. [Pass and time.] This word is used according to its original acceptation, not so much to express amusement, as occupation for the mind.

Bosham

"I likes evening school, 'tis such a pastime; but there's a passel of chaps that comes and döänt want to learn naun themselves, and wunt let any one else."

PAT. A hog-trough. Also called Tro or Trow.

PATHERY. Silly; applied to sheep which have the water on the brain. Sometimes 'Patherish,' or 'Puthery.'

PATTENS AND CLOGS, e. Lotus corniculatus. Also called pigs' pettitoes, and ladies' finger. Also God Almighty's thumbs and fingers, Butter-and-eggs.

PAUL. [Pal, Ang. Sax., a stake.] A division of tenantry land at Brighton, usually containing about the eighth part of a tenantry acre. Set out by a stake or post called a pall or pale.

PAT-GATE. A turnpike gate.

PEAKED, m. [Piqué, French.] Fretful: unwell.

"Weary seven nights, nine times nine,
Shall he dwindle, peak and pine."
– Macbeth. Act i. sc. 3.

PEASHALM. [Healm, Ang. Sax., stubble.l Pea-straw.

PECK. A pick-axe.

PECK. To use a pick-axe. To pick a hole.

These words illustrate the following evidence given by a witness in a case of manslaughter, –

"You see he pecked he with a peck, and he pecked he with a peck, and if he'd pecked he with his peck as hard as he pecked he with his peck, he would have killed he, and not he he."

PEEL, m. [Pelle, French, a shovel.]

A wooden shovel with a long handle, used for putting the bread into the oven. Also made of iron.

PEERT, m. Lively. "She just is a nice pleasant peert young lady."

PEEZE. To ooze out; to leak.

PEG-AWAY. To eat or drink voraciously.

In ancient times the liquor was handed round in a wooden vessel, marked at different distances from the bottom with pegs; each drinker in his turn drank as much as would reduce the liquor down to the next peg below; hence, to peg away, is to drink fast, so as to lower the liquor in the vessel very quickly.

PELL. A hole of water, generally very deep beneath a waterfall.

A broad shallow piece of water, larger than an ordinary pond The Pells at Lewes; Pells at Buxshalls, Lindfield; and other places.

PELL, e. To wash away the ground by the force of water.

PEN, m. A stall for a horse in a stable.

PENNOCK, PENNOLD or PINNOLD. A little bridge over a water-course; a brick or wooden tunnel under a road to carry off the water.

PENNY-RATTLE, w. Yellow rattle. R. crista Galli.

PERCER, w. [Perçer, French.] A piercer; a punch used by blacksmiths.

PERK-UP. To toss the head disdainfully.
"Verily
I sweat, 'tis better to be lowly born,
And range with humble livers in content,

Than to be perked-up in a glittering grief,
And wear a golden sorrow."
– King Henry VIII, Act ii, sc. 3.

PERRAMBLE. [corruption of Preamble.]
"He set to and punched into him without any perramble whatsumdever."

PEST. A common ejaculation.
"What the pest has become of the watering pot?"

PET, m. [Pett, Ang. Sax.] A pit.

With charcoal makers, colliers, the pet (pit) is built up of the bats of wood set round a central hole to be made into coal, the whole stack being the clamp.

PETER-GRIEVOUS, m. [Petit-grief, French, little grief.] Fretful; whining.
"What a peter-grievous child you are! Whatever is the matter?"

PETTIGUES, e. Troubles; vexation.
"She's not one as would tell her pettigues to everyone, but she's had as many as most for all that."

PHARISEES. Great uncertainty exists in Sussex as to the definition of this word according to its acceptation in the minds of country people, who always connect it with fairieses (their plural of fairy).

A Sussex man was once asked, "What is a pharisee?" and answered, with much deliberation and confidence, "A little creature rather bigger than a squirrel, and not quite so large as a fox," and I believe he expressed a general opinion.

Since writing the above, I find that polecats are called varies in Devonshire; so that possible the

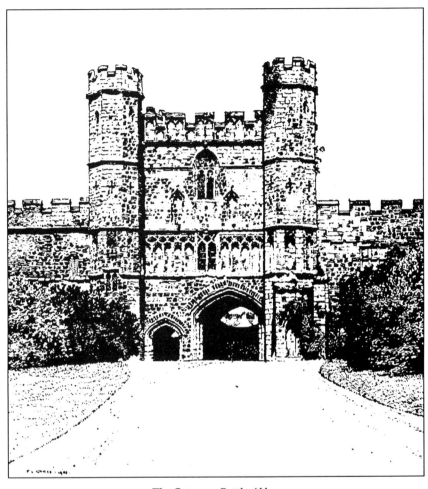

The Gateway, Battle Abbey

person who gave this answer had been brought in contact with some west-country folk and had heard the word from them. It is not Sussex.

PICKED, or PIKED, w. Pointed.

PICKPOCKETS, w. Shepherd's purse. Capsella bursa pastoris.

PICKSOME. Dainty. Fastidious; particular.

"She be that picksome and dentical."

PICK-UP. to overtake.

"I picked up the postmen between Selmston and Berwick."

PICK-UPON. To annoy.

"They always pick upon my boy coming home from school."

PIGEON-COVE, w. A dove cot.

PIG-MEAT. Fresh pork. By the word pork alone, salt pork is always meant.

PIGSCOT, w. A pigstye. A hog pound.

PIKER. (From pike, a highway or turnpike.) A gipsy or tramp. Particularly, a foot-slogging tramp.

PILLAR. A large thick pile of white (cumulus) clouds. They indicate thunder.

PILLOWBERE, w; and PILLOW-COAT, e., or PILLOW-TIE. A pillow case.

PILRAG, e. A field that has been ploughed up and neglected.

PIMPS, m. Small bundles of chopped wood for lighting fires.

PIPE-KILN, w. A framework of iron, in which long dirty clay pipes are put, and placed over a hot fire or in an oven, till they burn white and clean again.

PITCH, e. An iron stake for making holes in the ground for hurdles; called in West Sussex a folding bar.

PITCHER, m. The man who lifts and pitches the córn or hay up on to the wagon. Those who unload the wagons on to the stack or rick are called impitchers, or inpitchers.

PITHERED, m. Gummed-up.

"I've had such a terr'ble gurt cold, my eyes seem quite pithered-up o'mornings."

PIZE, e. A strong expression; thought by some to be connected with swearing by the pyx.

"What the pize have you got to do with it?"

PLAIN, m. Any piece of ground that is level, no matter how small it may be.

PLATE-BONE. The blade-bone.

PLATTY, e., or PLETTY. Uneven; usually said of a crop.

To say that "apples are very platty this year" would mean that there is a quantity in some places and none at all in others.

PLAW, e. A small wood; a plantation. As in Plawhatch. Ashdown Forest.)

PLOG.∞ To clog or hinder.

PLUCK, e. The lungs, liver and heart of a sheep or lamb.

PLUM-HEAVY. A small round cake made of pie-crust, with raisins or currants in it. The 'h' is always silent in this word in rustic use.

Dr. J. C. Sanger, of Seaford, when Government Surgeon at the Cape of Good Hope, was sent for to see an English settler. Reaching the house at tea-time, he joined the family at their meal, and on sitting down to the table he said, "You come from Sussex." "Yes," was the answer, "from Horsemouncies (Hurstmonceux), but how did you know that?" "Because you have got plum-heavies for tea," said the doctor," which I never saw but when I have been visiting in Sussex."

POACH, m. [Pocher, French, to thrust; poke.] To tread the ground into holes, as cattle do in wet weather.

"Mus' Martin's calves got into our garden last night; there was fowerteen 'an 'em, and they've poached the lawn about middlin' I can tell ye! Master will be mad!"
The word poacher evidently has the same derivation; the sports-man regards his game as his own,

but the poacher intrudes, or pokes into the property of another, as explained in Cotgrave. Or it might be derived from 'poke' (of the pig) – and mean one who "carries off game in a bag." – Johnson's Dictionary.

People frequently talk of poached eggs, as if they had been stolen, instead of delicately cooked (as they ought to be) in poches or bags of wire or muslin.

POAD-MILK, e. The first milk given by cows after calving. Also called Quail-milk.

POD. The body of a cart.

POINTING-STETHE, w. A small anvil or stithy.

POISON-BERRY, w. Black bryony. Tamus communis.

POKE, w. [Pocca, Ang. Sax., a pouch.] A long sack.

"To buy a pig in a poke" means to buy it in the sack and so to take a thing for granted without proper enquiry.

POLE-PULLER. The man whose business it is to pull the hop-poles out of the ground and lay them down for the pickers.

In former times, at the commencement of the hop-picking season, the pickers purchased a neck-cloth for the pole-puller. The article was of some showy colour, to make him more conspicuous in the hop-garden, and its purchase seems to have been attended with some convivialities, if we may judge from the following extract from the diary of Mr. Turner, –

"September 23, 1756. – Halland hop-pickers bought their pole-pullers nick-cloth and, poor

The ruined nave of Boxgrove Priory

wretches, many of them insensible."

POLLARD. Often said Pollards. The refuse siftings of flour, finer than bran and coarser than sharps.

POLT, e. A hard driving blow. The form pult occurs in early English.

POND-PUDDING. Another name for the Black-eyed Susan.

POOCH. To push or dig into anything.

POOCHER, m. An instrument used by thatchers.

POOK-HALE. Puck's Hall: the fairy's cottage.

A cottage at Selmeston goes by this name, and one of our numerous ghosts is still said to frequent the spot.

There are many farms and closes in Sussex which owe their names to having been the reputed haunt of fairies.

POOR. Thin. The proverb "as poor as a church mouse" is connected with this meaning of the word. When the numerous candles which adorned the altar, or were placed before shrines of patron Saints, were removed at the Reformation, the mice which formerly frequented the churches were starved out.

POPPLE, e. To bubble. A poppling sea is when the waves rise and fall with a quick sudden motion.

POSSNET, w. A skillet; a small saucepan. A Stusnet.

POT-HANGER, w. A hook shaped like the letter S on which the black pot was hung over the fire to boil.

POUD.* An ulcer; a boil.

POULTS, w. Beans and peas sown and harvested together.

POUND, m. [Ang. Sax. pund, a fold; pyndan, to pen up.] A small enclosure. A pig-stye is called a hog-pound, or pig-pound. A village pound was for enclosing any strayed animal.

POUNTLE, w. Honest reliable. Probably a corruption of punctual.

POWDERNG-TUB, m. A tub for salting meat. When ready the result was called powdered beef, etc.

"From the powdering tub of infamy,
Fetch forth the lazar kite of Cressid's
    kind."
– King Henry V, Act ii, sc. 1.

PRATT, w. The bar of a plough to which the traces are fastened.

PRAYERS-GOING, e. Service in church. In these days it means chapel-going rather than church going.

"We only have prayers-going once on a Sunday at our church."

PRAYING-BOOK, e. The Prayer Book.

PRENSLEY, m. [Corruption of Presently.] It and 'presently' are still used to mean 'at present' or now.

PRIMED. Half-tipsy. Overcharged with drink and ready to explode into any kind of mischief.

PRINT-MOONLIGHT, e. Very clear moon-light.

"He must have been primed to fall into the pond such a night as that was, for t'was print-moon-light.

PROG. A linch-pin.

PRONG, m. A hayfork with two speens.

PROPER. Thorough. Unexpectedly

The Refectory, Battle Abbey

good. Often said "Praper."
  "He's a proper old rogue!"

PUCKER. A fuss. Over-anxiety, with a little touch of ill-temper.

PUCKERED-UP, m. Shrivelled up with cold

PUCKETS.* Nests of catapillars.

PUDDING-CAKE. A composition of flour and water boiled; differing from a hard dick in shape only, being flat instead of round.

PUG. A kind of loam. Particularly the sticky yellow clay found in many parts of the Weald.

PULL. To summon before the magistrates.
  " 'E wer pulled up for poachin'."

PUMPLE-FOOTED. Club-footed

PURTY. [Corruption of Pretty.]

PURVENSION. Responsibility.
  "It is none of my purvension" means "I am not answerable for it."

PUTT-IN. To bury.
  "Master Hackleford is a man I always respacted, and if I knowed when he was a-going to be putt-in, I'd goo for sartin."

Q

QUAINT. [For acquainted.]

QUALITY, w. This word occurs in old parochial account books for a kind of tape.

QUARTERING, w. The wooden framing of a house, the upper story of which is made of wood-work covered with tiles.

QUEER, m. To puzzle.
"It has queered me for a long time to find out who that man is; and my mistus she's been quite in a quirk over it. He döánt seem to be quaint with nobody, and he döánt seem to have no business, and for all that he's always to and thro', to and thro', for everlastin'."

QUERN, w. [Cwéorn, Ang. Sax., a mill.] A hand-mill to grind malt.
"Are you not he,
that frights the maidens of the villag'ry,
Skim milk, and sometimes labour in the quern?"
– Midsummer Night's Dream, Act ii, sc. 1.

QUEST, e. To give tongue like a hound.

QUICK, w. Pregnant.
"Faith, unless you play the honest Trojan, the poor wench is cast away; she's quick."
– Love's Labour Lost, Act v, sc. 2.

QUICK. [Cwic, Ang. Sax., living.] Alive.
"I thought that the sheep was dead when first saw it, but I found it was quick still."

QUICK. To hurry; used actively and reflexively. "I'll quick him fast enough if he doesn't quick himself a little more."

QUICK. An expression applied to the sands when they are insecure from not being sufficiently firm and dry.
Quick sand is live sand; active. The Brighton boys call it live sand. "You should not ride on the sands so soon after the tide has turned, for they are sure to be quick and shifting."

QUID. A cud.

QUIDDY, e. [Que dis tu? French.] What do you say?
"Quiddy? I didn't hear what you said."

QUILER-HARNESS, w. The trace harness.
In fact, quiler harness is worn by the Thill-horse or wheeler, and trace harness by the leaders.

QUILERS, or QUOILERS, w. Part of the harness of a cart horse; the breeching. Its function is to hold back the cart or wagon when going downhill and for backing.
The word means queller. (Cwellere, Ang. Sax., a killer, a queller.)

QUILL, w. A spring of water (Variation of Well.)

QUILLY, m. The roughness of the skin produced by cold, sometimes described as goose-flesh; or goose-skin.

QUILT. To claw and pound with the paws, as cats do upon a carpet; also callcd "making-bread." When the cat makes bread it is a sign of rain.

QUIRK, m. A fuss; a whim; a fancy.
"I may chance have somc odd quirks and remnants of wit broken on me, because I have railed so long at marriage . . . When I said I should die a batchelor, I did not think I should

Shoyswell, near Ticehurst

live till I were marry'd."
– Much Ado About Nothing, Act ii, sc. 3.

QUONT, or QUANT.
  [Compare contus, Latin.] A barge-pole, with a divided end; also a punt pole.

QUOTTED. Satiated; glutted.

QUYER. Enquire. – On a journey –
  "I thought 'twas time to quyer."

R

RABBITS, e. An ejaculation. "What the rabbits! Why, it's never you out in such weather as this, surelye!"

RABBIT'S-MEAT, m. Wild parsley. Anthriscus sylvestris.

RACKETTING-RIDDLE, w. [Hriddel, Ang. Sax., a sieve.] A cane-bottomed sieve.

RACKON, m. [Corruption of Reckon.] "The fire burns middlin' rash; I rackon 'tis because 'tis so frosty."

RACK-UP. To supply horses with their food for the night. I.e. to put the food or fodder up into the rack.

RAD [Corruption of Rod] The shaft of a cart; a measure of 16½ feet, by which distance is more frequently measured than by yards, as elsewhere. Forty rods – 1 furlong, ⅛th of a mile.

RADDLES. [Diminutive of Rod.] Long supple sticks of green wood interwoven between upright stakes to make a hedge.

RADDLE or RATTLE AND DAB. Frame-work of timber filled in with wattle and mortar, or with wattle and mud.

RADDLE-FENCE, e. A hedge made with raddles.

RADES, w. The rails of a wagon.

RADICAL, e. Tiresome; Disobedient. A radical is a bad, mischievous lad.

"He's that radical that I döánt know whatever'll become an him. I've told him adunnamany times not to ride on the rads, but 'tis no use what you says to him."

RAFTY, e. Very.

RAFTY2, w. Ill-tempered; difficult to manage.

RAGGED-JACK, e. Scotch kale.

RAGGED-JACK, e. Ragged robin. Lychnis flos-cuculi.

RAKE, e. The sea is said to rake when it breaks on the shore with a long grating sound.

RAKE. "As lean as a rake" is a common proverb among Sussex people, who use the word in the same sense as in the following passage –
"Let us revenge this with our pikes, ere we become rakes; for the gods know, I speak this in hunger for bread, not in thirst for revenge."
– Coriolanus, Act i, sc.. 1.
"As lene was his horse as is a rake." – Chaucer, Prol. I. 287.

RAMP, e. To grow rapidly and luxuriantly.

RANK. Smoke. (This was probably a printer's error for Rauk.)

RANN.† (Run, in the sense length.) A division of a net. nets are ordered to be "in deepness two ranns, every rann fifty moxes deep."

RAP-AND-RUN, or RAP-AND-REND.* [Icel. hrapa, To rush head-long.] To seize and plunder; to seize hold of everything one can.

RAPE. [Hreppr, Icelandic.] A division of a county comprising several hundreds. The Normans divided the county of Sussex into six rapes – Hastings, Pevensey and Lewes, in East Sussex; Bramber, Arundel, and Chichester, in West Sussex. Each of these rapes had a castle near the coast, and an available harbour at its southern extremity, and formed what was called "a high road to Normandy."

RARE, m. [Hrére, Ang. Sax., raw.] Underdone.

RASH. [Ræsc, Ang. Sax., a flash.] Fierce and clear; said of a fire in frosty weather.

"His rash fierce blaze of riot cannot last,
For violent fires soon burn out themselves."
– Richard Il., Act ii. sc. 1.

RATHE.∞ Early; as rathe in the morning. (Ray.)

RATHER-RIPE. [Hræth, Ang. Sax., early.] The name of an apple which ripens early. Generally spelt "ratheripe", and pronounced "rath'ripe."

RATTLEBONE. Worn out; tumbling to pieces.

RAVE-CART. A common cart fitted with raves.

RAVES. Two frames of wood which are laid on the top of a wagon in such a way as to meet in the middle and project on all sides beyond the body of the vehicle, so as to enable it to carry a larger load.

REAFE. [Reafian, Ang. Sax., to seize; seize upon.] To anticipate pleasure; to long for the accomplishment of anything; to speak continually on the same subject.

REARING-FEAST. A feast given to the workmen when the roof is reared or put on the house.

REBELLIOUS. [Corruption of bilious.]
· "I should be very much obliged for a few of them rebellious pills."

RECKON, m. To suppose. A Sussex man uses the expression, "I

New Shoreham Church

reckon" as often as an American uses "I guess."

Usually pronounced "rackon", but sometimes said "riggin."

"Did put the yoke upon us; which to shake off,
Becomes a warlike people, whom we reckon
Ourselves to be."
– Cymbeline, Act iii. sc. 1.

RECOLLECTS, e. Memory.

"I quite lost my recollects, and the doctor he redeemed it was through along of the fever."

REDEEM, m. [Corruption of Deem.] To consider; to give an opinion.

REEK, m. [Reác, Ang. Sax., smoke.] Fog or mist rising from the marsh.

"You common cry of curs! Whose breath I hate
As reek of the rotten fens."
– Coriolanus, Act iii. sc. 3.

REEVE. [Ge-réfa, Ang. Sax.] A bailiff; an officer of the lord of the manor.

REFUGE, e. To separate the inferior sheep or lambs from the flock.

REFUGE. [Corruption of Refuse.] Worthless: unsaleable.

RENDER. To give the finishing coat of plaster to a wall.

REVE, or REVES, m. Rent or tithes. The fishermen at Brighton are liable to pay six mackerel as reves each time they return from mackerel fishing.

REYNOLDS. "Mus Reynolds" is the name given to the fox. When I was first told that "Mus Reynolds come along last night" he was spoken of so intimately that I supposed he must be some old friend, and expressed a hope that

he had been hospitably received. "He helped hisself," was the reply; and thereupon followed the explanation, illustrated by an exhibition of mutilated poultry.

RHEUMATICS. A woman once said to me, "There's so many new complaints now-a-days to what there used to be; there's this here rheumatism there's so much talk about. When I was a gal 'twas the rheumattics, and I döänt know as there's much odds in it now – naun but if you wants to cure the rheumatism you wants a lot of doctor's stuff; but for my part, if ever I be troubled with the rheumattics (and I be quite eat-up otherwhile) I goos out and steals a tater, and carries it in my pocket till the rheumattics be gone."

RIB-LADE, w. The bar on the side of a wagon parallel with the lade.

RICE, w; RICE-HEADING, e. [Hrîs, Ang. Sax., a twig.] Underwood cut sufficiently young to bear winding into hedges or hurdles.

RICKSTEDDLE. m. [Hreac and Stéde, Ang. Sax., a rick place.] An enclosure for corn or hay Ricks.

RICKSTEDDLE, w. A wooden frame placed on stones on which to build the ricks, in order to keep the ricks ventilated, the bottom hay dry and preventing rats and mice getting in.

RIDDER e. [Hridder, Ang. Sax.] An oblong coarse wire sieve used with a blower for winnowing corn, the ridder being moved to and fro on a stake in front of the blower.

RIDDLE, w. [Hriddel, Ang. Sax.] A large sieve for sifting wheat in a barn ... or for sifting ashes. Sieves generally are called riddles.

RIDE, m. Any bridle-road, but generally a green way through furze or woodland.

RIDE, e. A rut, or wheel mark.

RIDE, m. To be a burden. "I didn't want to ride the club, so I declared off."

RIDE-HORSE, e. A saddle-horse.

RIDES, e. The iron hinges on a gate by which it is hung to the post and so swings or rides.

RIDGE-BAND, e; RIDGER; RIDGE-STAY, w., or RIDGE-TIE. Back-band. [Hryg, Ang. Sax., the back.] That part of the harness which goes over the saddle (pad) on the horse's back, and being fastened on both sides, supports the shafts of the cart.

RIDGE-BONE. The weather boarding on the outside of wooden houses, common in Sussex and Kent. Some times called Ridge-laves.

RIFE, w. A ditch on the moorland. (Rythe.) Also a level for draining. E.g. Pagham rife, from which the high tide is excluded by the sluice, and which drains at low tide.

RINGLE. [Diminutive of Ring.] A small ring, such as that put into the snout of a pig to prevent him from rooting up the floor of his sty. I find among the manorial customs the following regulation, – "It is also ordained that every one do yoke or ring his hogs before the feast of St. Michael the Archangel next, and the same keep so yoked or ringed until the feast of St. John the Baptist then next following, under pain of forfeiting to the lord, for every hog, for every week, 3s.

4d.

RINGLE, m. To put rings in hogs' snouts. And when this is done the hogs are ringled. Ringled also means married.

RIP. To reap. The sickle is called the rip-hook.

RIPE. [Ripa, Latin.] A bank or sea-shore. A village in East Sussex is called by this name. Ripe also means bank, shore, edge and Ripe is on a small ridge above marshy ground. It was probably coastal when it got its name. In Norman times Lewes was on the fore-shore.

RIPIERS. [Icel., hrip, a basket.] Men from the coast who carry baskets of fish to inland towns and villages. The word rip is still used in Scotland for a basket.

RISING, e. Yeast.

ROBBUT. [Corruption of Rabbit.] Sometimes pronounced as broadly as robert.
"Robbuts! Ah, I lay you never see such a plááce for robbuts as what ourn is! I never should have beleft, without I'd seen 'em in my garden, that there was so many robbuts in the wurreld. Why they be ready to eat us up alive!"

ROKE. [Roec, or Reác, Ang. Sax., smoke.] Steam; mist.

ROMNEY MARSH. There is a saying in East Sussex that the world is divided into five parts – Europe, Asia, Africa, America, and Romney-marsh.

ROOKERY, m. A disturbance; a fuss and chattering. "I never knew of a wedding but what the women-folks made a middlin' rookery over it."

ROOSTER. The common cock. The

Mount Street, Battle

Americans invariably call cocks by this name.

ROSSEL-FENCE, w. The same as raddle-fence.

ROTHER, w. [Hryther, Hruther, Ang. Sax.] A horned beast.

ROUGH. Passionate; angry.

"Mus Moppet he'll be middlin' rough if he sees you a throwing at he's rooster."

ROUNDEL. A circle; anything round.

ROUND-FROCK. A loose frock or upper garment of coarse material, generally worn by country-people over their other clothes. A white round frock is considered mourning, and when worn (as I have sometimes seen it) under a greatcoat, the effect is by no means good, particularly when viewed from behind.

ROUPEY. [Connected with the Ang. Sax., Hreop from hrépan: or the Icelandic, hropja, to scream out.] Hoarse.

ROWENS, m: or ROUGHINGS, e.

The latter grass which comes after mowing, and is frequently

The Ouse at Piddinghoe

left for cattle to eat in the winter when it becomes coarse and rough.

RUBBER. The stone used for whetting the scythe. Also called a Bristle-bat. Putting the keen edge on to the scythe is called sharping.

RUBBIDGE. Rubbish; especially weeds in a garden.

RUDY, m. Rude.

"They boys! They boys! They be so rudy."

RUE, w. [Rue, French, a street.] A row; a hedge-row; rough land; a rough lane; a Shaw; usually spelt Rew.

RUNAGATE. A good-for-nothing fellow.

"There let him sink, and be the seas on him!

White-livered runagate, what doth he there?"

– Richard III, Act iv. sc. 4.

RUNDLET. A small circle. [Diminutive of Roundel.

RUNT, w. To grub up the roots of trees by drawing them out of the ground in a way which does not much disturb the soil.

RUSTY, w. Unruly: ill-humoured.

RYTHE, w. [Rithe; Ang. Sax., a fountain; well; rivulet.] A small stream; usually one occasioned by heavy showers of rain.

S

SABBED. Wet; saturated; sopped

SAD. Sodden; heavy; said of bread which has not risen well. And of beer that is flat.

SAFE, w. Sure; certain.
"He's safe to be hanged "

SAG. [Connected with Sægan, Ang. Sax., to cause to descend.] To fit badly; to hang down on one side; to subside by its own weight or an overload.
"The mind I sway by, and the heart I
    bear,
Shall never sag with doubt, nor shake
    with fear."
– Macbeth, Act. v, sc. 3.

SALIMOTE, m. The court of the lord of the old manor of Brightelmston in 1656 was described as the Salimote Court.

SALLET. A salad. (As ballet for ballad.)
"Sunday, May 13, 1764. Myself, Mr. Dodson and servant at church in the morn. We dined on a calf 's heart pudding, a piece of beef, greens and green sallet. Mr. Hartley came to bring me a new wigg. Paid him in full for a new wigg £1 l5s., and new-mounting an old one, 4s."
– Diary of Mr. Turner, of East Hoathly.
Shakespeare uses the word, –
Clown. – "Indeed, sir, she was the sweet marjoram of the sallet; or, rather the herb of grace."
Lafeu. – "They are not sallet herbs you knave, they are nose herbs."
– All's Well that Ends Well, Act iv. sc. 5.

SALLY, e. [Salig, Ang. Sax.; Salix, Latin.] A willow.

SALTS, e. Marshes near the sea, overflowed by the tides. (E.g. Salts Farm, Lancing.)

SAPE. [Sæp. Ang. Sax.] Sap.

SARE. [Searian, Ang. Sax., to dry.] Withered; dry; said of wood.
"Burn ash-wood green,
'Tis fire for a Queen:
Burn ash-wood sare,
'Twool make a man swear."

SARMENT. A sermon.
"I likes a good long sarment, I doos; so as when you wakes up it aint all over."

SATTERED, m. Thoroughly soaked. (Probably a corruption of Saturated.)
"I was fair sattered."

SAUCE, m. (Pronounced Sass.) Vegetables; but generally used of cabbages. The Americans speak of garden-sass.
"I reckon I sháánt have no sass at all this year, all through along on account of the drythe."

SAYE. Serge or woollen cloth. – Cheeseworth Inventory, 1549.

SCAD, m. A small black plum which grows wild in the hedges.

SCADDLE, m. [Scæthig, Ang. Sax. hurtful.] Wild; mischievous; thievish. The Anglo-Saxon word sceatha has the same double meaning (1) a robber; thief; (2) an adversary. Applied to a truant boy, or a cow which breaks through hedges, or a cat which steals.

SCADE. Harm; mischief.

SCALY, w. Inclined to steal.

SCAMBLE, w. To make a confusion of anything.
"The scambling and unquiet time
Did push it out of further question." –
King Henry V., Act i. sc. 1.

SCAR, e. [Possibly connected with Icel., skár, open, exposed.] Exposed to.

"Our house lays quite scar to the sea."

SCARCEY, m. Scarce. Also used in Kent.

SCONCE. [Schans, Dutch, a sconce.]

A socket fixed in a wall for holding a candle.

SCORING-AXE. An axe used to chip round the stem of a tree, previous to falling (i.e. felling it).

SCORSE. To exchange. Like scrunch for crunch, this word is corruption of the Old English word corse, which means to barter, exchange, etc.

"This catel he got with okering,
And spent al his lif in corsing."

i.e., "This cattle he acquired by usary, and led all his life in bargaining." – Old Metrical Homilies.

Spenser also used the word, –

"And therein sat an old old man, half blind,
And all decrepit in his feeble corse,
Yet lively vigour rested in his mind
And recompenst them with a better scorse;
Weak body well is changed for minds redoubled forse."

– The Faerie Queene, Book II, Cant. ix. 5.5.

The following instance will illustrate the modern use of the word, –

A gipsy boy, with whom I was on friendly terms, used to travel about this part of the country selling trumpery brooches and ornaments. As he was one day exhibiting the contents of his basket, I was surprised to see half-a-dozen onions loose among the jewelry. "What," I said, "do you sell onions too?" "No, sir," he replied, "but I scorsed away a pair of diamond ear-rings for these few onions, with a lady down at the cottage yonder."

SCRATCH-ALONG. To pull through hard times.

"What with otherwhiles a day's turmut-hoeing, and otherwhiles a day's tan-flawin', and otherwhiles a job of gardenin', I've just managed to scratch-along somehows."

SCRAZE. [Connected with graze.] To scratch, or rather to scratch and bruise at the same time.

"She was climmin' up after some scads and fell down and scrazed her knees."

SCRIER, or SCREER, e. A high standing sieve which is used for cleansing corn from dust and other rubbish; sometimes called a screen.

SCROW, or SCROWSE, e. [Connected with the Old English word crus, wrathful.] Angry; dark and scowling.

SCRUMP, e. [Scrimmian, Ang. Sax., to wither up.] Anything undersized.

In Hampshire a small shrivelled up apple is called a scrumpling.

SCRY, e. To sift corn through a scrier.

SCUD. Driving rain; mist.

SCUFFLE, e. An outer garment worn by children to keep their clothes clean; a coarse apron for dirty work.

SCUFFLE-PLOUGH, w., or SCUFFLER. A skim; a shim', a horse-hoe.

Boxgrove Priory from the south

SCUPPIT. A wooden shovel used by maltsters and hop-driers. Shaped like a large dustpan that is used in the house.

SCUTCHETT,* w., or SCRUTCHELL. The refuse of wood

SCUTTY, m. A wren; also called a cutty, juggy and kitty.

The Sussex small boys have a Small Birds Act of their own, which is found sufficient for the protection of all birds which they consider entitled to protection, and commands much more respect and obedience than a recent Act of Parliament.

"Robins and wrens
Are God Almighty's friends;
Martins and swallers
Are God Almighty's scholars."

SEAM. [seam, Ang. Sax.] Eight bushels, or a horse load.

SEAN, or SEINE. [Seine, Old French, still used in France.] A very large net used for catching mackerel or herrings.

SEAR. [Searian, Ang. Sax., to dry up.] Dry; withered; burnt up by the sun.
"My way of life is fallen into the sear, the yellow leaf."
– Macbeth, Act v. sc. 3.

SEASON, m. Ground in good condition.

SEE. Used always as the perfect for saw . . . sometimes 'seed '.
"I never see such larmentable poor ground as this here. I've been diggin' it over to get a season to plant a little onion seed, but I shan't make naun an't."

SEED-CORD.* [Connected with the Dutch word korf, a basket.] A wooden vessel in which the sower carries the seed.

SEED-LIP, m. [Sæd-leap, Ang. Sax.] A basket for seed; a seed cord. The same as lepe or side-box.

SEEDSMAN, m. The foreman of the farm, whose business it is to sow.

SEN. Since.
The Sussex word is the older form, and is traced to the Ang. Sax.

siththan, which became sin, sen, or sithen, from the last of which was formed sithens, whence since.

"I haven't been over to Selmeston not sen I was seedsman at Mus Allwork's. Ah ! he was a set sort of a man, he was, and no mistake."

SESSIONS. A great deal of business; a fuss.

"There's always such sessions over lighting up the church in winter time."

SET. Obstinate; self-willed; determined

SET-OUT. A disturbance.

"There's been a pretty set-out up at the forge."

SETTLE. [Setl, Ang. Sax., a seat.] A wooden seat with a back and arms.

"He fell down off the settle and scrazed his nose and made as much set-out as though he'd been killed."

SEVERALS, m. Portions of common assigned for a term to a particular proprietor; the other commoners waiving for a time their right of common over them.

"My lips are no common, though several they be."
– Love's Labour Lost, Act ii. sc. 1.
Ayscough gives the following note on this passage.: –
"This word (several), which is provincial, means those fields which are alternately sown with corn, and during that time are kept several or severed from the field which lies fallow and is appropriated to the grazing of cattle, not by a fence, but by the care of the cowherd or shepherd, and in which the town bull only is allowed to range unmolested.

SEW, e., or SUE. [Sychu, Welsh, to dry up; cognate with Latin siccare.]
To drain land. Or a pond.

SEW, e. An underground drain. Hence sewer. Also a main drainage channel.

SEW, w. A cow is said to be gone to sew when her milk is dried off.

SHACKLE, w. To idle about; to waste time; to be very busy about nothing.

SHACKY. Shabby; ragged.

SHADE. [Shard.] A piece of broken tile or pottery.

SHAG, w. & m. A cormorant. Also called a Raven.

"As wet as a shag," is a common expression, taken from the idea of a cormorant diving frequently under the water.

SHARD, e. A gap in a hedge. This word, like shade, is derived from the Anglo-Saxon sceard, which means (1) a shard; (2) a division.

SHARP. * The shaft of a cart.

SHARPS. The finest refuse siftings of flour.

SHATTER, m. A number or quantity.

"There's a tidy shatter of hops this year.

SHAUL, or SHAWLE. A wooden shovel without a handle, used for putting corn into a winnowing machine. This word is a variation of shool or shovel.

"I, said the owl,
With my spade and showl."

SHAW, e. A small hanging wood. Also called Rew, or Rue. Ray defines it as "a wood that encompasses a close."

SHAY. A faint ray of light. A flash of light; a halo.

In Kent the word means a general likeness, and seems to correspond to the Sussex bly.

A man who was trying to describe to me a fearful apparition which he had seen in Firle Park, said, after much cross-examination, that it passed quite close to him in the form of an enormous white horse, and there was a bluish shay. I should myself have supposed that a horse and shay was a sufficiently common object of the country not to have excited undue influence, but on this occasion the appearance was so overwhelming that the man was ill for several days.

SHEAR, e. A spear, as an eel-shear.

SHEAT, e. A young hog of the first year.

SHEEP-CAGE. A framework out of which sheep eat their hay, etc., in a strawyard.

SHEEP-LEAZE,† or TEG-LEAZE.

The right of turning out one sheep to feed on a common.

SHEER. [Scir, Ang. Sax., clear, white.] Smooth and shiny, as flesh which is swollen.

SHEERES. The true Sussex man divides the world into two parts. Kent and Sussex forms one division, and all the rest is "The Sheeres." I have heard China and Australia both described as in the sheeres; but I confess that I was somewhat startled at being told that I was myself "a man as was well acquaint with the sheeres,

Brede Place from the south

and had got friends in all parts of this world and the world to come." This statement was meant as a compliment, but when I came to consider it afterwards, I was not sure that it was altogether complimentary to some of my friends.

SHEERE-MAN. A man who comes from the shires (and not necessarily sure of a favourable reception in Sussex.)

SHEERE-MOUSE. A field mouse. A shrew-mouse. Properly speaking a shrew is a vole, not a mouse.

The country people have an idea that the harvest-mouse is unable to cross a path which has been trod by man. Whenever it attempts to do so it is said to be immediately struck dead. This accounts (they say) for the numbers which on a summer's evening may be found lying dead on the edge of the field footpaths without any wound or apparent cause of death.

SHEERE-MOUSE. An epithet of derision applicable to a sheere-man. The phrase "the sheeres" is found in many other parts of England, and is generally expressive of a certain degree of depreciation. In Shropshire the manufacturing districts are spoken of as "down in the shires."

SHEERE-WAY, e. (Shire-way). A bridle-way.

SHELL-FIRE. Phosphorescent light from decaying matter; called also fairy sparks.

SHELVE, e. To throw manure out of a cart by raising the fore-part so that the bottom may shelve or slope.

SHIM. [Schim, Dutch, a shade or ghost.] A glimpse of anything.

"I thought I saw a shim of the carpenter going by the gate just now, but I'm not sure."

SHIM, e. A narrow strip or glimpse of white on a horse's face.

SHIM. A horse hoe for cleaning the ground between rows of beans or hops.

SHIMPER. [Scimian, Ang. Sax., to shine or shimmer.] To shine brightly.

SHINGLES. Small wooden tiles made of split oak used for roofs, steeples, etc.

There are several church spires in Sussex covered with these shingles.

SHIP, m. Sheep.
Seldom used in the singular.

SHIRTY. Easily offended. A man who has quickly lost his temper is said to have got his shirt out . . . i.e., he has taken off his coat as if to fight.

SHOD. [Perfect of Shed.] spilt. This word is correct, the Anglo-Saxon past tense being sceód

"I sent him up to fetch a little beer, but he shod half of it bringing of it home."

SHOES AND STOCKINGS, m. Lotus eorniculatus. A wild flower of the cypripedium genus (Holloway) called in East Sussex "pattens and clogs" or "butter and eggs."

SHOG. The core of an apple.

SHOKE, m. [Scoc, Ang. Sax., perfect of scacan, to shake.] The original form of shook.

"He shoke his fistes in my face, he did!"

SHOOKED, e. Shook.

"I shooked in my shoes to hear what words he used."

SHOOLER, e. An idle, lazy fellow; described as "a man who goes about with his boots undone."

SHOOT, w., or SHUT. A young growing pig.

SHOOT. A gutter round a roof for shooting off the water.

SHORE, m. To shelve off; to cut off evenly.

"If the road was better shored at the sides the water wouldn't lay so much as what it does."

SHORE. [Schoren, Dutch, to prop up.] A prop, a support.

SHORN-BUG, m. [Scearn, Ang. Sax., dung; scearn-wibba, a shorn-bug.] A beetle. To eat shorn-bugs for dinner is a proverbial expression for the extremity of poverty.

SHORT, m. Out of temper; unable to give a civil answer.

"Guvnor were tidy short wi' me, short as moss 'e wur."

SHORT. Tender.

A rat-catcher once told me that he knew many people who were in the habit of eating barn-fed rats, and he added, "When they're in a pudding you could not tell them from a chick, they eat so short and purty."

SHOTTERS.† Boats of six to twenty-six ton burden, used in the mackerel fishery.

SHOVE, e. To put the loose corn into cops or heaps, that it may be more conveniently taken up.

SHRAPE, e. To scold.

SHRAVEY.* A loose sub-soil, some thing between clay and sand.

"The ground is more shravey up here than it is down by the pond."

SHRIEVY, e. Unravelled; having threads withdrawn.

SHROGS, e. The refuse trimmings of hop-plants; also called chogs.

SHRUCK, e. Shocked.

SHRUCK, e. Shrieked.

An old woman who was accidentally locked up in a church where she was slumbering in a high pew, said, "I shruck till I could shruck no longer, but no one comed, so I up and tolled upon the bell."

SHUCK. Another form of the perfect tense of the verb to shake.

SHUCK, e. To undress; to shell peas. etc.

SHUCK, m A husk or pod.

SHUKISH or SHUCKY. Unsettled; applied to the weather.

"Better take yer brolly, it be shuckish like."

SHUN. To push.

"He shunned me off the pavement."

SHUT, v;. A young pig; also called a sheat or shoot.

SHUT-OF, m. To be rid of.

"Once he gets indoors, you'll be troubled to get shut an' him; I dunno but what you'd best shun him out of the fore-door at oncest." Pronounced Wunst.

SIDEBOARDS, w. Rails fitted on the top of the sides of a wagon, so as to admit of the addition of an extra load.

SIDELANDS, w. The outside parts of a ploughed field, adjoining the hedges, where the plough has been turned, running parallel with

Rudgwick

the lands or warps.

SIDY.* Surly; moody.

SIEVER, e. All the fish caught at one tide.

SILT, e. Sand or mud deposited and left by the tide or a flood.

SILT-UP. To become so choked-up, with mud or sediment of any kind, as to stop the passage of water in a ditch or the bed of a river.

SIMPLE, e. Unintelligible, or stupid.

"Will you be so good as to send mother another book? for she says this one is so simple she can't make it out at all."

SISSEL, m. The usual pronunciation of thistle.

SIZZING. Yeast or barm. It is probable that this word may have its origin in the sound made by beer or ale in working.

SKEELING.* The bay of a barn; the

side of a garret or upper room, where the slope of the roof interferes with the upright.

SKEP, [Scep. Ang. Sax., a basket.] A beehive, or the straw hackle placed over it for protection.

SKEP, e. A hat; a broad flat basket made of rushes or straw.

SKICE. To run quickly and slily, so as to avoid detection.

"I just saw the top of his skep as he skiced along under the hedge."

SKID. To check a wheel going down hill.

SKID-PAN. The iron used for skidding.

SKIM-COULTER. That part of a plough which goes in front to take off the turf.

SKINNY, w. Mean; inhospitable.

SKIP, e. A small wooden or metal vessel for taking up yeast.

SKIRMISH, m. To run about in a

mischievous manner.

"It's no use to try and keep a garden tidy as long as the children are a skirmishing about over the flower borders."

SKITTERWAISEN, w. From corner to corner. Probably a corruption of Catawise.

SKIVEL, w., or SKIVER. A skewer. In the west, dogwood, of which skewers are made, is called skiver-wood.

SKREEL, e. To scream.

SKROW. Surly; ill-tempered

SLAB, m. A rough board; the outside cut of a tree which has been sawn up in planks.

SLABBY, m. Dirty; wet and slippery; greasy; sticky.
Also said Slobby and Slubby.
"Make the gruel thick and slab."
– Macbeth, Act iv. sc. 1.

SLAM. To do any work in a slovenly manner.

SLAP, m. In good condition; hearty.

"I don't feel very slap this morning."

SLAPPEL.* A portion; a large rough piece of anything.
SLAT, m. A slate.

SLATES, m. The pods of peas, etc.

"The peas seem to be out in bloom a long time before they hang in slates this year."

SLAVVEN. A large piece.
"I give 'im a slawen o' puddin'."

SLAY, or SLEIGH. A slope.

SLEECH, e. Mud or sea-sand used as manure. The sediment deposited by the river Rother is called sleech.

SLICK. [Slíkr, Icel.; smooth.] To comb the hair; to make it sleek. This word is used frequently in America in this sense.

SLIM. [Slim, Dutch. Schlimm. German, bad; sly.] To do work in a cunning deceitful manner.

SLING. A cow or ewe which brings forth her young prematurely is said to sling her calf or lamb.

SLIPE. To take off the outside cover from anything; especially used of removing the bark from trees.

SLIRRUP. To lap up any liquid noisily.

SLIT.* [Connected with the Dutch word Sluiten, to shut or lock.] To thrust back the lock of a door without the key.

SLIVER, w. [Slífan, Ang. Sax., to cleave.] A slice.
"Sliver'd in the moon's eclipse."
– Macbeth, Act iv, sc. 1.

SLOCK, e. [Corruption of slack.] Loose; ill fitting.

SLOCKSEY, e. Slovenly. (Probably connected with the word slack.)

SLOMMAKY, m. Untidy; dirty. Sometimes spelt slummocky.

SLOP, m. [Slóp, Ang. Sax.] A short, full-made frock, of coarse material, worn by men over their other clothes; it reaches to the waist, where it is fastened by a band.

SLUB, SLAB, or SLOB. Thick mud; used as slush is elsewhere.

SMEECH, m; or SMUTCH, e. [Sméc, Ang. Sax., smoke, vapour.] A dirty black sort of smoke or mist. Any bad smell made by burning, but not otherwise.

In the west of England the word means a stench, and is applied to the smell of the snuff of a candle.

SMOCK-WINDMILL. A windmill boarded down to the ground, as opposed to a post-mill. So called from its similarity in appearance to a smocked round frock or smock.

SMOLT, e. [Smolt, Ang. Sax., smooth.] Smooth and shining.

SMOORN, e. To smear.

SMUTCH, e. To smudge. Also same as Smeech, a dirty smoke. "What, hast smutched thy nose!" – Winter's Tale, Act i. sc. 2.

SNAG, or SNEG. The common snail.

With respect to this word, which I had been inclined to derive from the Anglo-Saxon snæg-el, Mr. Skeat informs me that it is the old original word of which snæg-el is the diminutive; hence snag is not derived from snæg-el, but vice versa. The children say, –
"Snag, snag, put out your horn,
And I will give you a barley corn." The snail is also called Hodmandod.

SNAP-PLOUGH, w. A plough with two wings, so fixed as to snap or move from one side to the other, though only one projects at a time.

SNETHE, m; or SNEAD, w. [Snæd, Ang. Sax.] The long handle of a scythe. The short handle is called a neb.

SNICKER, m. [Snikken, Dutch, to gasp.] To sneer: to laugh inwardly.

SNIGGLER, m. A slight frost.

SNOB, m. [Connected with Icel., snápr, a fool and knave.]
A travelling shoemaker: a cobbler.
In the neighbourhood of

Burwash it is considered a most unfavourable description of a stranger to say that he is "a broken down snob from Kent."

SNOULE, e. A small quantity of anything. Used in Norfolk for a short thick cut from the crusty part of a loaf or a cheese.

SNUDGE, m. To hold down the head; to walk with a stoop looking on the ground as if in deep thought.
"There they goos, acrost the Common, snudging along."

SNUFFY, m. Angry. A common nickname for a testy person.
"Old snuffy came mudging along here just now, and wanted to borrow a few Brussels sprouts, but I lent him a brockylo once and never got it back again, so I warn't agoing to be took in a second time."

SOCK, m. A blow.
"I'll give that old sow-cat o' yourn a sock aside the head if I catches her in my house agin!"

SOCKISH, m. (Probably a variation of Suckish.) Requiring to be petted and nursed; said of a child.

SOCK-LAMB, m. A lamb brought up by hand. Also called a hob lamb.

SOCKLE, m. To suckle.

SODGER, m. A red herring; literally a soldier.
The sirloin of a jackass, stuffed with sodgers, is a Sussex man's definition of coarse, univiting food.

SOLLY, e. A tottering or unstable condition.
"That cart-lodge of Mus' Dicksey's is all of a solly; t'wunt

least but a very little while longer afore it comes down."

SOME-ONE-TIME, m. Now and then; occasionally.

"Some-one-time I goos across to the Chequers, but döánt make no rule of it."

SOMEWHEN. At some time.

SOOKLAND or SOKELAND, e. [Soc. Ang. Sax., a right or privilege of court, or of taking action at court.] (Soke of Peterborough.) A name in the manor of Wadhurst for assartland.

SOOR, m. An exclamation expressive of surprise.

SOOR. [Corruption of Swore.]

"When I told him that the calves was got into the green house, he jumped up and soor that dreadful that I was all of a shake."

SOPS-AND-ALE. A curious custom formerly prevalent at Eastbourne, which has fallen into disuse in the present century. The senior bachelor of the parish was elected by the inhabitants to the office of steward, and had committed to his charge a damask napkin, a great wooden bowl, twelve wooden trenchers, a dozen wooden knives and forks, two wooden candle-sticks and two wooden sugar basins.

Whenever a matron within the parish increased her family, it was the duty of this official to go to the church door on the Sunday fortnight after the interesting event, and there publicly proclaim that sops and ale would be provided that evening at a certain house agreed upon, where the following arrangements were made. Three tables were placed in some convenient room, one of which was covered with the damask table cover and furnished with a china bowl, plates, and silver handled knives and forks; the bowl was filled with biscuits steeped in wine and sweetened with fine sugar. The second table was also covered with a cloth and decently provided with knives, forks and china, and a bowl containing beer-sops sweetened with fine sugar. The third table had no cloth, was furnished with the wooden trenchers, candle-sticks, etc., and had its wooden bowl filled with beer-sops sweetened with the coarsest sugar. After evening prayers the company assembled at the house of their entertainer, and were placed in the following order:– The persons whose wives had presented them with twins sat at the first table, and were addressed as "benchers"; those whose partners had blessed them in a less degree were ranged round the second table; while those who were married but childless, were placed with the old bachelors at the third table. Various toasts were given, and the company always broke up at the temperate hour of eight, "generally very cheerful and good tempered" – Sussex Archaeological Collections, vol. xiii. p. 228.

SOSS-ABOUT, e. To mix different things together; generally applied to liquids.

"To soss" in the North means to go about in the dirt.

SOSSEL. To make a slop.

SOW. A word used among the old Sussex iron-workers for a weight of 2,000 lb.

SOW-CAT, m. A female cat.

SOW-WAPS. The queen wasp.

In some parts of the county a reward of sixpence is of offered for each sow-waps killed in the spring.

SPACE. A measurement of three feet. Spaces and rods are almost the only terms of measurement I have ever heard used by country people.

SPACE. To measure ground.

SPALT, e, or SPOLT. [Connected

St Ann's Church from Southover

with the Dutch spalten, to split.] Split; brittle; decayed. Applied to timber ... that breaks carroty as horse-chestnut does.

SPALTER, w. To split or chip off.

SPANNEL, m. To make dirty foot marks about a floor, as a spaniel dog does.

"I goos into the kitchen and I says to my mistus, I says ('was of a Saddaday), the old sow's hem ornary, I says. Well, says she, there aint no call for you to come spanneling about my clean kitchen any more for that, she says; so I goos out and didn't say naun, for you can't never make no sense of women-folks of a Saddaday."
Shakespeare uses the word in the sense of dogging the steps,–
"The hearts that spaniel'd me at heels."
– Antony and Cleopatra, Act iv. sc 10.

SPANNER, w. A wrencher; a nut screw.

SPAN-NEW. Quite new. Very new and smart.

SPAR, or SPARRER. [Spére, Ang. Sax., a spear.] Called also Spick, Speek and Spelk. A stick pointed at each end, and doubled and twisted in the middle; used by thatchers to secure the straw on the roof of stack or building.

SPARR. [Corruption of Sparrow, as Barr for Barrow.]

SPARTACLES. [An invariable corruption of Spectacles.]

SPAT. A slap or blow.

SPATS, m. Leather gaiters reaching above the knee. Sometimes said 'Pats.'

SPATTLEDASHES, m. Short leather gaiters not reaching much above the ankle. The real word is 'Spatterdashes' and is contracted to 'spats.'

SPEAR, m. The sting of a bee. Also the tongue of a snake or lizard which are said to 'sting.'
A bee is always said to bite in Sussex.

SPEAR. To sprout up out of the ground.
"Soonsever the peas begins to spear, the meece and the sparrs gets holt an' em."

SPELTS. Iron toes and heels for boots.

SPENE, or SPEEN. The prong of a pitchfork, or other forked implement.

SPENES. [Spana, Ang. Sax.] The teats of a cow.

SPET. Spit.
"The old cat set there, and there she set, and spet and soor and went on all the whole time."

SPICE. [Espéce, French.] A slight attack of illness.
"I had a spice of the ague last week, and I döánt want no more of him, for all that they says " 'tis worse not to have him than 'tis to!' "

SPILE, w. A spigot.

SPILT. [Spillan, Ang. Sax., to spoil.] Spoiled.
"She shod the milk all over her, and spilt her new frock."

SPILWOOD. Refuse of wood; wood split (or spoilt) by the sawyers.

SPINNEY. A thicket; a small plantation.

SPIT, m. As much earth as can be taken up at once with a spade.

SPIT-DEEP, m. As deep as a spade

goes in digging.

SPLASH, m. To bank up a hedge.

SPLASH, e., or SPLISHER, m. To lay a live hedge.

SPONG;, e. To cobble; to work in a rough clumsy way with a needle.

SPRACKISH, w. Smart and active.

SPRAY-WOOD. Faggots of brush wood used in the ovens.

SPREAD-BAT, e., or SPREADER. A wooden bar used to keep the chains apart from rubbing the horses' legs and sides when drawing a plough or harrow, or in any trace harness.

SPROG.* A linch-pin. Or lynsepin. Also called a prog.

SPRONG, e., or SPRONK, m. The roots of a tree or a tooth.

SPRONKY, m. Full of roots.

"Ah! I guv' old Muz' Tweazer the biggest job o' tooth-pulling ever he had! It took him purty nigh two hours! and he said he'd never seen such a tooth all his days, to goo so fur down nor yet to be so spronky."

SPRUG, e. To smarten.

SPRY, e. Gay, cheerful. Vivacious.

A word frequently used in America, meaning "in good health."

SPUD. A light garden tool with a long handle for cutting up weeds. Also an ordinary garden fork.

SPUDDLE, m. To use a spud. To fork over without digging.

"I be gettin' in years and can't do no more than just doddle about the ground and spuddle up a few weeds."

SQUAB. A young unfledged bird.

SQUACKETT, m. To quack like a

duck.

"I thought Mus' Reynolds was about last night, the ducks kep all on squacketting so."

SQUAT, w. To indent or bruise anything by letting it fall.

SQUAT-BAT, e. A piece of wood used for stopping a wheel while the horses are at rest on a hilly road.

SQUATTY, w. Said of meal that has fermented.

SQUENCH, or SQUENCE, m. [Corruption of Quench.]

Blacksmiths "squench" hot iron in the water.

SQUINNEY. To squint; to pry about.

SQUIRM. To wriggle like an eel.

STAB. A small hole in the ground which the rabbit secures her young litter.

STABBLE, e. To make a floor dirty by walking on it in wet or muddy shoes.

STADE, e. [Stede, Ang. Sax.] A shore where ships can be beached; a landing place. A staith.

STALDER. [Stælan, Ang. Sax., to place.] The stool on which casks are placed in a cellar.

STALLAGE, m. or STOLLAGE (Same as Stalder.)

STALLED, e. Fired; satiated.

"Ain't you fairly stalled of waiting?"

"I think the old dog has stalled himself now, for he found a stab out in the held and eat the lot."

STAMMERS. The fresh shoots of a tree which has been cut back.

STAM-WOOD, m. [Stam, Dutch, a stem; a trunk of a tree.] The roots of trees, stubbed or grubbed up.

STANDING. A stall at a market or fair.

STARK, e. [Stere, Ang. Sax., rigid.]
Ground is said to be stark or starked up, when the surface has dried very quickly after rain.

STARKY, e. Flinty.
"The land is very starky."

START. An excitement; a fuss.
"There's been a pretty start up at the forge this morning! Fighting and all manner."

When a Sussex man is at a loss for words to describe events or ideas of a somewhat discreditable nature, he gets out of the difficulty by using the phrase "all manner!" If he wishes to describe great profusion and plenty, he says "there was everything of some thing and something of every-thing, as the saying is;" but where he gets the saying from I have no idea.

STATESMAN, m. An estates' man; a man who owns a few acres of land and farms them himself.
The general condition of such persons is that their property is mortgaged, and with much harder work they are worse off than ordinary labourers.

STEALE. [Stela, Ang. Sax., a handle.]
The handle of most agricultural implements.

STEAN. To pave a road with stones; to line a well or a grave with stone or brick.
The Steine, at Brighton probably, derives its name from this word.

STEAN, m. To mark out a field for ploughing, which is usually done by placing large stones to show the lines.

STEDDLE. [Stathol, Ang. Sax., a basis.] The wooden frame-work placed on stones or other support, on which corn stacks are built.

STEDDLE, m. A small side table, or a temporary arrangement of boards and trestles.

STENT, m. A portion of work appointed to be done in a set time.

STEW. A pool in which fish are kept for the table.

STILL. Quiet; respectable.
"He's a nice still man."

STILL-WATERS. Distilled waters. There is generally an old woman in every village who is a notable distiller of waters, which are in great request as domestic medicine.

STILTS. Crutches.
It is rather surprising to be told that a person is such a complete cripple that he can only walk with stilts.
If infirm and uses sticks he is said to "walk on two bats."

STINT, e. Shabby; undergrown.

STITHE, w., or STITHY. An anvil.
"If his occulted guilt
Do not itself unkennel in one speech,
It is a damned ghost that we have
　　seen;
And my imaginations are as foul
As Vulcan's stithy."
– Hamlet, Act iii, sc. 2.

STIVED-UP, m. Crowded.
"We were all stived-up in one room. There was four families, one in each corner, and a single man who slep' in the middle. I put up with it as long as I could, but when the single man began to take in lodgers I couldn't stand it no longer."

Arundel

STIVER-ABOUT. (The i is pronounced as in shiver.) To stagger.

STOACH, e. To trample ground as cattle do in wet weather.

STOACH-WAY, e. An expression used at Rye harbour for the channel which runs through the sand lying between the pier-head and the deep water at low tide. At Selsey they would call that a "swatch-way."

STOACHY. Dirty: muddy.

STOCKY, m. Strong; stout; well grown.

STOCKY, m. Headstrong; saucy; wilful; generally said of girls.
"Since nought so stockish, hard, and
    full of rage,
But music for the time doth change
    his nature."
– Merchant of Venice, Act v. sc. 1.

STODGE, e. Thick mud.

STODGE, m. A fuss.
"He's always in such a stodge; if he's got to goo anywhere's he always wants to be off two hours too soon."

STOKE. To stir the fire; hence the word stoker.

STOLT, e. Stout; strong; generally said of fowls.
"The chickens are quite stolt."

STOMACHY, m. Proud; obstinate.

STONE. A weight of eight pounds.

STOOD. m. Stuck fast.
An old man told me, "I've seen a wagon stood in the snow on the road from Selmeston to Alciston, and they never moved it for six weeks."

STOOL-BALL. An old Sussex

134

game similar in many respects to cricket, played by females. It has lately been revived in East Sussex by the establishment of stool-ball clubs in many villages, which not only provide good exercise for young ladies who might otherwise become lazy, but also promote kind, social intercourse among all classes. The 'elevens' go long distances to play their matches; they practice regularly, and frequently display such perfection of fielding and wicket-keeping as would put most amateur cricketers to shame. The rules are printed, and are as keenly discussed and implicitly obeyed as those of the Marylebone Club.

The game is thus alluded to in Poor Robin's Almanack for 1740, –
"Now milkmaid's pails are deckt with flowers,
And men begin to drink in bowers;
Sweet sillabubs, and lip-loved tansey,
For William is prepared by Nancy.
Whilst hob-nail Dick and simp'ring Frances
Trip it away in country dances;
At stool-ball and at barley-break,
Wherewith they harmless pastime make."

STOP, e. A rabbit-stab; probably so called because the doe stops up the entrance when she leaves her young.

STORM-COCK, or SREECHER. The missel thrush.

STOT, w. A young bullock.

STRAND, m. A withered stalk of grass, one of the twists of a line.

STREALE.• [Stræl, Ang. Sax.] An arrow.

STREET. In Sussex a road is called a street without any reference to there being houses beside it; but I am quite unable to say why some roads should be distinguished from others by being so called. (A street originally meant a paved road, from the Latin strata via.)

STRIDE, m. A long distance.
"I döänt exactly know the name of the place he's gone to, but I know 'tis a middling stride into the sheeres."

STRIG. The foot-stalk of any fruit or flower. As of currants, etc.

STRIKE. A smooth straight piece of wood used in measuring, to strike the loose corn which lies above the level of the rim of the bushel.
In old inventories "a bushel and strike" usually go together.

STRIKE-PLOUGH, m. A plough used for striking out the furrows.

STRIVES, m. Rivalry.
"Sometimes I think those people must dress so for strives, to see who can be smartest."

STROD. A forked branch of a tree. A catapult strod, like the letter Y.

STROMBOLO. (Possibly connected with the Dutch stroomballen, stream or tide balls.)
"Pieces of black bitumen highly charged with sulphur and salt, found along the coast. Called thus at Brighton, doubtless from the Flemings settled in the town. The stones have been used for fuel, and Dr. Russell applied the steam to scrofulous tumours." – Durrant Cooper's Sussex Glossary.

STUB, e. The stem which is left standing out of the ground after a tree has been cut down.

STUB, e. To stub a horse is to lame him by letting him tread on stubs of underwood in a cover.

STUB, m. To grub up trees with their roots.

STUB, m. To pluck chicken clean after their feathers have been pulled off.

STUCKLING. An apple-pasty made thin in the shape of a semi-circle, and baked without a dish.

STUD, m; STUDY, e. A state of thoughtfulness.

"He seems all in a stud as he walks along."

STUMP, w. A stump of hay is an item frequently found in farm inventories in West Sussex. It means the remains of a round stack, most of which has been cut away.

STUPE, e. Stupid; dull.
An old schooldame thus described the progress of a pupil (aged 5): –

"He's that stupe that he can't tell 'A's' from 'V's', and he actually döánt know the meaning of 'Verily, verily!' "

STUSNET. A skillet; a small saucepan. A Posnet.

SUDDENT, m. Suddenly.

SUE, e. To drain land; also a drain.

SUENT, e. Pleasant; agreeable.
Moving freely and easily whether of an animal or of a machine.

" 'E be very suently inclined to 'er I reckon."

SULLAGE. [Souiller, French to soil.] Any filth or dirt of the nature of a sediment.

SUMMER, e. The beam which supports the bed or body of a wagon.

SUMMER AND WINTER, w. To have summered and wintered a person is to have known him at all seasons and under all circumstances, both good and bad.

SUPPOSE, m. This word is used not to express conjecture, but certainty.

SURELYE. There are few words more frequently used by Sussex people than this. It has no special meaning of its own, but it is added at the end of any sentence to which particular emphasis is required to be given, and numerous examples of its use will be found in illustrations of other words in this dictionary.

SUSHY, e. [Séche, French, dry.] In want of water.

"I never knowed such a dry time; we're as sush as sushy."

SUSSEL. A disturbance; an impertinent meddling with the affairs of other people.

SUSSEX-MOON. A man sent on in front with a lantern fastened behind him. Also the large lanthorns used on the broad wheeled wagons.

SUSSEX-PUDDING. A compound of flour and water made up in an oblong shape and boiled. There is a moment when it is first taken out of the saucepan, when it can be eaten with impunity; but it is usually eaten cold, and in that form I believe that it becomes the foundation of all the ills that Sussex spirit and flesh are heir to. It promotes a dyspeptic form of dissent which is unknown elsewhere. It aggravates every natural infirmity of temper by the promotion of chronic indigestion, and finally undermines the constitution; for the first symptom of the decay of nature which a Sussex man describes is invariably that he can't get his pudding to set. It was often cut in slices and eaten when cold with treacle especially for breakfast.

SWAD, or SWOD, e. A bushel basket, generally used in selling fish.

SWADE. The leather strap of a spinning-wheel.

SWADING-IRON, w. An instrument used in a blacksmith's forge.

SWALLOCKY, e. A term applied to the appearance of clouds in hot weather before a thunder-storm.

SWANK, w. A bog; a dell or damp hollow.

SWANK, m. Small beer.

SWAP, m; To reap corn and beans.

SWAP-HOOK, m. The implement used for swapping.

SWARLY or SWORLY. Ill-tempered; usually applied to animals.

SWARVE, e. To fill up; to choke with sediment. To silt up.
"Our ditch is quite swarved up."

SWATH. [Pronounced swarth.] A row of cut grass or corn as it is laid on the ground by mowers or swappers.
"And there the strawy Greeks, ripe
   for his edge,
Fall down before him, like the
   mower's swath."
– Troilus and Cressida, Act v, sc. 6.

SWEAL. [Swélan, Ang. Sax., to kindle.] To burn the hair; to singe a pig.

SWELT. [Sweltan, Ang. Sax., to die.] Hot; faint.
"Like a swelt cat, better than it looks."

SWINGE. [Swingan, Ang. Sax.] To flog.
"I will swinge him well when I catches him."

SWINGEL. [Swing-el, Ang. Sax., That part of a flail which beats the corn out of the ear. (The 'g' is soft.)

SWORKE. [Corruption of sulk.] To be angry and surly.

SWORLE. To marl like a dog.

SWYMY. [Swimmy.] Giddy; faint. A person who isn't seasick but feels bad is swymy or swymy-headed.
"I felt so swymy that I was obliged to get up and go out of church."

137

T

TACHENERS.∞ Young men employed in the fishing boats. (Possibly so called from being taken to learn the trade.) Or from teach. This is the same word as Takeners.

The spelling Tacheners is from the Brighton Custumal of 1580.

TACK. A peculiar flavour; a strong, rank, nasty taste.

TACK. A path or causeway.

TACKLE. Working implements; machinery of any kind.

TACKLE. Distasteful or other food or drink.

"I calls this here claret wine about the poorest tackle ever I táásted."

TAG. e. A sheep of the first year. A teg.

TAIL-WHEAT, m. The inferior grain which is left after the corn has been winnowed.

TAKENERS, m. Persons taken to learn a trade; young men employed in fishing-boats at Brighton.

TALK THIN. To talk in a low voice.

"He talk so thin that no-one can't scarcely hear what he says."

TALWOOD, w. [Tailler, French, to cut.] Wood cleft and cut into billets for firing.

TAN-FLAWING. Taking the bark off trees, the bark itself being called tan.

"If I can get a job of tan-flawing I shall make out very well."

TAVORT. Half a bushel.

TAWER. [Tawian, Ang. Sax., to prepare hides.] A fellmonger; a leather dresser.

("Tawere, a tawer," Bosworth's Anglo-Saxon and English Dictionary.)

TEAM, w. [Téman, Ang. Sax., to propagate.] A litter, or a number of young beasts of any kind.

"I have got a nice team of young pigs here."

TED, m. To spread hay; to shake out the new mown grass.

Nowadays the hay which has lain in swath until one side is dry, is "tedded" to dry the other side. Hence the implement used is the Tedder.

TEDDIOUS. Fretful; difficult to please.

TEDIOUS. Excessive; very. Pronounced 'Tejus.'

"I never did see such tedious bad stuff in all my life."

TELL. [Tellan, Ang. Sax., to count.] To count.

"Otherwhiles I be forced to tell the ship over six and seven times before I can get 'em right."

Shepherds tell their sheep letting the flock run through between two hurdles at a time.

TELLER, m; TELLAR; or TILLOW, w. [Telgor, Ang. Sax., a branch.l A young oak tree.

TEMPERSOME. Hasty-tempered

TEMPEST. When the wind blows roughly it is said to tempest.

"It tempestes so as we're troubled to pitch the hay upon (up on) to the stack anyhows in the wurreld."

TEMPESTY, w. A gale of wind

TEMPORY. [corruption of temporary.] Slight; badly finished.

"Who be I? Why I be John Carbury, that's who I be! And who be you? Why, you aint a man at all, you aint! You be naun but a poor tempory creetur run up by contract, that's what you be!"

TENANT-ACRE. Mr. Durrant Cooper gives the following account of this allotment:–

"The proportion between the tenantry and the statue acre is very uncertain.The tenantry land was divided first into laines, of several acres in extent, with good roads, some sixteen feet wide between them; at right angles with these were formed, at uncertain intervals, tenantry roads, of some eight feet in width, dividing the laines into furlongs. In each furlong every tenant had a right to his proportion, which was set out for him, not by fixing any superficial quantity, but by measuring along the line of the tenantry road of each furlong a certain number of feet to each paul, the number of feet being the same, whatever was the depth of the furlong; thus, if the furlong, for instance, consisted of what is called a hatchet-piece, something like three quarters of a square, the part where the piece was two squares deep would contain double the superficial contents of the portion at the other end, where the measurement next the road would be similar but the depth only one half."
Sussex Glossary.

TEND. To watch.

"He can't sing in church no more, for he goos to work rook-tending, and he comes home of nights that hoarse that you can't hardly hear him speak."

TERRIER. [Terre, French, land.] A survey and register of land.

Two terriers were made at Brighton in the last (18th.) century; the first in 1738, the second in 1792, by Thomas Budgen.

TERRIFY. (Usually pronounced tarrify.) To tease; to annoy.

"These here fleas tarrifies me tarrible."

TESSY, w. Angry. [Probably a

Pevensey Castle

139

corruption of festy.]

THAT. So.

"I was that tired I didn't know how to bear myself."

THICK-OF-HEARING. e. Slightly deaf.

"Old woman, old woman, will you go
    a shearing?
Speak a little louder, sir, I'm rather
    thick of hearing.
Old woman, old woman, shall I kiss
    you very sweetly?
I thank you very kindly, sir, I hear
    you quite completely."
– Old Sussex Rhyme.

THICK-MILK, m. Hot milk thickened by the addition of a few spoonfuls of flour and sweetened.

THILL-HORSE, w; or THILLER. The shaft horse.

"What a beard thou hast got. Thou hast got more hair on thy chin than Dobbin my thill-horse has on his tail."
– Merchant of Venice, Act ii. sc. 2.

THILLS, w. [Thil, Ang. Sax., a plank.] The shafts of a wagon or cart. Also called Rods and Sharps.

THREADDLE. To thread a needle.

"Open the gates as wide as wide,
And king George go through with his
    bride.
It is so dark, we cannot see
To threaddle the tailor's needle."
– Children's game.

THRO. Fro. To-and-thro is always used for to-and-fro.

"He goes to-and-thro to Lewes every Tuesday and Friday."

THROT, m. The throat.

THROW. [Through.] A thorough fare: a public way. The four-throws is a point where four roads meet. Carfax.

THROW. To cut down trees.

TICKLE-PLOUGH, w. A plough with wooden beam and handles.

TICKLER, e. An iron pin used by brewers to take a bung out of a cask.

TIDY, m. A child's pinafore, which keeps the dress tidy.

TIFFY. Touchy; irritable. (A tiff, a slight quarrel.)

TIGHT. Drunk.

Either Sussex beer must be very strong or Sussex heads very weak, for however drunk a man may have been he will declare that he did not take more than a pint, and all his friends will make the same assertion.

TIGHTISH. Well in health.

"I'm pretty tightish thank you" is not a very common expression, because it is not considered genteel to be in perfectly good health; and to say "How well you are looking" is by no means taken as a compliment. I suspect that the height of gentility is not reached till a person dies outright, and then of course it is only reflective, and the relations take credit for it.

TIGHT-UP. [Variant of dight, from dihtan, Ang. Sax., to dress.] To clean; to put in order.

"To tight oneself up" is to dress or put on clean clothes.

TILLOW, w. (See teller.)

TILTH, m. [Tilth, Ang. Sax., culture.] The condition of arable land That which is tilled.

"He's a man as always keeps his ground in good tilth."

TIME OF DAY, m. "To pass the time of day" is to greet a person passing on the road.

"I döant know any more of him than just to pass the time o' day."

TIMMERSOME, e. Timid

A boy, who recently stated as a valid reason for not attending evening school that he was afraid that the pharisees would interrupt him on his way home, was excused by his mother on the ground that he was "that timmersome that he couldn't abear to go out after dark."

TINKER, w. To mend anything clumsily. To botch.

TIPPED, m. Pointed.

TIPTEERERS, w. Mummers who go round performing a sort of short play at Christmas time. Or Tipsheers or Tipsteers.

TIP-TONGUED. To talk tip-tongued is to talk in an affected manner.

"She talks so tip-tongued and gives herself such airs."

TIRE. Flax for spinning. (Probably obsolete, but frequently found in old parochial accounts.) Also spelled tyre.

TISSICK, m. A tickling, faint cough.

"Punch cures the gout, the cholic and the phthisic,
And it is agreed to be the very best of physic."
– Old Song.

TIVER, w. Red ochre used for marking sheep.

TO-AND-AGIN, m. Backwards and forwards.

"She doddles to-and-agin."

TOKEN', e. A present. From the old phrase: "A token of love."

"My lad's brought me such a nice token from Rye."

TOKEN, m. An apparition.

A woman who had asked me to write to the War Office for tidings of her son, whose regiment was in India, came to me a few days afterwards to say that she was sorry she had given me so much trouble, as it was no use to make any enquiries about her son for he was dead, and she knew it because she had seen his token, which had walked across the field before her and finally disappeared over the stile. It was useless to reason with the woman, or to attempt to comfort her by reading her the reply from the War Office that her son was well. It was not till he returned home and in his own person refuted the evidence of the token that her confidence in it was at all shaken.

TOM. Any cock bird, as a tom-turkey or a tom-parrot.

"I bought two hens and a tom off old Mis Cluckleford, but I döant know as I shall make out much with 'em, for they döant seem none of 'em inclined to lay."

TOM-BACCA. Traveller's joy. Clematis vitalba; also called boys'-bacca, because the boys cut the small wood in pieces to smoke like cigars . . . and call it also "smoking cane."

TOMMY, m. Bread.

TONGUES, e. Small soles; probably so called from their shape.

TOOK-TO, e. Ashamed; vexed.

"I was quite took-to when you come in, for I hadn't had time to tight-up all day."

TOP-OF-THE-HOUSE. A person who has lost his temper is said to be up-a-top-of-the-house .

"You says anything to him he's

up-a-top-of-the-house   drackly minut."

TORE-GRASS, m. [Also spelt toar grass.] Tare-grass.

The long old grass which remains in pasture during the winter.

TO-RIGHTS, m. Completely; perfectly.

"I had my little boy into Lewes to get his likeness taken a Saddaday, and the man took him to-rights, and you'll say so when you sees it."

TOSS, e. [Tas, Ang. Sax., a mow of corn.] The mow, or bay of a barn into which the corn is put to be thrashed.

TOT, m. A bush; a tuft of grass. Same word as Toat.

"There warn't any grass at all when we fust come here; naun but a passel o' guff old tots and tussicks. You see there was one of these here new-fashioned men had had the farm, and he'd properly starved the land and the labourers, and the cattle and everything, without it was hisself."

TOT. e. A brood of chicken; a covey of partridges. And a small child that can only totter.

TOTHER-DAY. If pronounced t'-otherdy, means the day before yes-terday.

This expression is correct, because in Early English other invariably means second, and the day before yesterday is the second day reckoning backwards. It is remarkable that second is the only ordinal number of French derivation; before the thirteenth century it was unknown, and other was used instead of it. – Archæologia Cantiana, vol. ix.

TOTTY-LAND, e. [Totian, Ang. Sax., to elevate.] High-land, frequently on a side of a hill; used at Hastings.

TOVET, e. [Two fats; a fat, or vat, is a peck.] A measure of half-a-bushel.

TO-YEAR, w. This year, as to-day is this day.

TRACK. A pathway across a field.

TRADE. Anything to carry; such as a bag, a dinner basket, tools or shop goods.

"He's a man as has always got such a lot of trade along with him."

TRADE, e. Household goods; lumber.

TRADES. [Treads]. The ruts in a road.

"You will never get your car-riage down that laine, for it can't take the trades," i.e., it cannot run in the ruts.

TRAIN, m. To boil down fat for lard.

TRAMP, e. Gin and water.

TRAPE. To trail; to drag along the ground. "Her gown trapes along the floor."

TRAPES-ABOUT. To run about in an untidy, slovenly manner; to allow the dress to trail on the ground.

A Sussex maid describing to another servant how her mistress went to Court, said, "And as soon as ever they sees the Queen they lets their dress tails trapes, because it ain't manners to hold 'em up."

TRAVERSE or TRAVASE, or TRAVIS. The place adjoining a blacksmith's shop where horses are shod. Also the partition between stalls in a stable.

Mr. Turner had an adventure in a traverse, which he thus records in his diary:– "1758. Sept. 27. In the morn my brother and self set out for Eastbourne. We dined on a shoulder of lamb, roasted, with onion sauce – my family at home dining on a sheep's head, lights, etc., boiled. We came home about 10 p.m., but not sober. Being very drunk, my horse took the wrong way, and ran into a travase with me and beat me off."

From this it would appear as if Mr. Turner had entertained his horse as liberally as himself!

TREFT, m. A trivet.

TRENCHER. [Trancher, French, to cut off.] A wooden plate on which to cut up meat or bread.

TRENCHERMAN, m. A feeder. A good trencherman is a hearty eater.
"He's a very valiant trencherman, he hath an excellent stomach."
– Much Ado About Nothing, Act i. sc. 1.

TRESSLES. The dung of sheep or rabbits, or hares.

TRIG, w. To place anything behind a wheel to prevent a carriage from slipping back on a hill.

TRIPET, w. A wicket gate.

TRUCK. Rubbish; odds and ends.
"There's too much truck about the floor for the house ever to look tidy."

TRUG. [Trog, Ang. Sax., trough.] A strong basket made of split wood, used for gardening. Invented at Hurstmonceux.

TRULL. [Corruption of trundle.] To bowl a hoop.

TRUNDLE-BED, w. A low bed on small castors, trundled under another in the daytime. A truckle-bed.

TRUNK, e. To under-drain land.

TRUSSING-BEDSTEAD, w. [Truss, Old English, to pack up.] A camp bedstead which can be packed for travelling.

TRUT. A hassock or footstool.

TUCK A pinafore worn by children.

TUCK-APRON, m. A long apron which is fastened round the neck and waist.

TUCKERS. § Small boat of about three tons burden, used in fishing for plaice.

TUCK-SHELL.* A tusk.

TUG. A carriage for conveying timber.

TUGS. Iron chains which fit into the hames and shafts.

TUMBLE-DOWN GATE, m., or STILE GATE. A gate on a towing path so constructed that horses may pass over it while one end is pressed down. It recovers its position through being weighted at the opposite point. Also called Clatterdown gate.

TUNNELL, w. A funnel.

TURMUT, m. [Corruption of turnip.] Often "Durmut."
" 'Twas the worst year I ever knowed for a job of turmut-hoeing, for there warn't no turmuts for anyone to hoe."

TURN-WRIST PLOUGH. [Pronounced turn-rice, and sometimes so spelt in inventories.] A plough with a moveable mould-board, which turns up the

The Ouse at South Street, Lewes

second furrow on to the first.

TUSHES, m. Tusks; long teeth.
"O, be advised! thou know'st not
    what it is
With javelins point a churlish swine
    to gore,
Whose tushes never sheathed he
    whetteth still,
Like to a mortal butcher, bent to kill."
– Shakespeare. Venus and Adonis.

TUSSICK, m. A tuft of rank grass.

TWEEN-STICKS, w. Sticks which
are used to keep horses' heads
apart when working two abreast.

TWELVE-MONTHING. A yearling
calf.

TWIT. To taunt; to tease.
"And twit with cowardice a man half-
dead."
– Henry VI, Act iii. sc. 2.

TWITTEN, w. (Now used all over
Sussex.) A narrow path between
two walls or hedges, or wall and
hedge, usually leading from one
street to another.

TWO, e. To be at two is to quarrel.

TWORT, e. [For thwart, a corruption
of the Ang. Sax., thweor, perverse;
froward] Pert and saucy.
    "She's terrible twort – she wants
a good setting down she do; and
she'll get it too. Wait till my master
comes in!"

TYE, m. A common, a large open
field.

144

U

UNACCOUNTABLE. A very favourite adjective which does duty on all occasions in Sussex. A countryman will scarcely speak three sentences without dragging in this word.

A friend of mine who had been remonstrating with one of his parishioners for abusing the parish clerk beyond the bounds of neighbourly expression, received the following answer:

"You be quite right, sir: you be quite right. I'd no ought to have said what I did, but I döán't mind telling you to your head what I've said a-many times behind your back – We've got a good shepherd, I says, an excellent shepherd, but he's got an unaccountable bad dog!"

UNBEKNOWNST. Unknown.

"All I can say is, if he comes here, it's quite unbeknownst to me."

UNDERBACK. A large open vessel in a brewhouse, which is placed under the mash-tun.

UNFORBIDDEN, e. [Unforboden, Ang. Sax., undaunted.] Daring; disobedient.

UNKED. [Uncwyde, Ang. Sax., solitary.] Lonely; dreary; dismal.

UNKED. Having the appearance of evil; betokening bad weather.

UNLUCKY. Always in mischief.

UP. To get up.

"Soonsever he comes in at the foredoor his missus she ups and pulls his hair."

UP-A-TOP-OF-THE-HOUSE. In a rage.

"He's so hot headed, he's up-a-top of-the-house in a minut."

UPPISH. Pettish; out of temper; easily provoked.

" 'E was that uppish I went out."

UPSET. To find fault; to interfere with; to attack.

UPSTANDING. Upright; honourable.

"They're such an upstanding, down-sitting family, you won't find their match, search England through."

USAGE, w., or USUALS. Provisions given to workmen besides their wages, called also 'lowance (allowance).

V

VAIL. A present given to a servant over and above wages (like the French pourboire). The word is contracted from avail, and originally meant an advantage.

"Welcome shall they be;
And all the honours, that can fly from us,
Shall on them settle; you know your places well;
When better fall, for your avails they fell."

– All's Well that Ends Well, Act iii. sc.1.

VALIANT, w. [Vaillant, French.]

The Arun at North Stoke

East Mascalls, before restoration

Stout; well-built. Also very much. "What did you think of my friend who preached last Sunday, Master Piper?"

"Ha! he was a valiant man; he did just stand over the pulpit! Why you béant nothing at all to him! See what a noble haunch he had!"

VALLERS, or VOLLERS. Fallows. Spelt vallowes in Humphrey's inventory, 1697.

VENT, e. A place where several roads meet, generally pronounced went.

VERT. [Vert, French.] Green. Still retained in the names of fields, as The Lower Vert Field, at Selmeston.

VIVERS. [Viviers, French.] Fish ponds.

VLICK, w. To smooth the hair.

VLOTHERED, e. Agitated; flustered. Moithered.

"I was so vlothered I didn't know what to be at."

VOLLER, or VOLLO W, m. A fallow field.

VOOR, m., or VUR. A furrow. Contracted as barr for barrow.

W

WANT, w. An abbreviation of warrant.

"He wunt give ye naun I want ye."

WANTY, w. [Wamb-tíge, Ang. Sax. a belly band] The girth which is fastened to the thills of a cart, and, passing under the horse's belly, prevents the cart from tilting back.

WAPSEY, m. Spiteful; waspish.

"These bees of yours are terr'ble wapsey."

WAPS-HYME, w. A wasp's nest.

WARP. A piece of land consisting of ten, twelve, or more ridges, on each side of which a furrow is left to carry off the water.

WARP, e Four herrings, i.e., in telling or counting them when landed two in each hand.

WASE.* A small bundle of straw.

WATER-COWEL, w. A large wooden tub. A Cowell.

WATER-TABLE. A low part on the side of a road, or a small cutting across a hill-road to carry off the water.

WATTLE. [Watel, Ang. Sax,] A hurdle.

WEALD. [Weald, Ang. Sax., a forest or the Wild. The name given in Sussex to the large woodland tract of country which exter ds from the Downs, with which it runs parallel to the Surrey Hills. It was formerly an immense forest, called by the Britons Coit-Andred, and by the Saxons Andredes-weald – Durrant Cooper.

WEAN-GATE. [Wæn geát, Ang. Sax.] A wagon or wain gate.

WEAN-HOUSE. [Pronounced Wen hus.] A wagon shed.

WEAN-YEAR-BEAST, w. A calf weaned during the current year.

WEEZE, e. [Wæs, Ang. Sax., water.] To ooze.

WENT, e., or VENT. A Partways. A crossway. A place where several roads meet. By contraction from four-five-etc.-wents. Went strictly is a road or lane.

"Just as gate (from the verb go) means a street in Old English, so went (from the verb wend) means a lane or passage." – Pegge's Alphabet of Kenticisms.

WEST-COUNTRY-PARSON, e. The hake, so called from the black streak on the back, and abundance of the fish along the western coast.

WET. To wet the tea, is to make tea. Or rather to infuse the tea in a little boiling water before adding the volume of boiling water

To wet the bread. is to mix the water in the flour. To "wet the top brick" is a bricklayers' celebration.

WHAPPLE-GATE. A gate on a whapple-way.

WHAPPLE- WAY. A bridle way through fields or woods, where horses can go but carts cannot. Some times written Wapple.

WHEELS, m. A hand cart.

"I can get my wheels through whapple-gate, and that often saves me a journey fetching wood."

WHIFFLE, m. To come in gusts.

"I see there had been just rain enough to whiffle round the spire whiles we was in church."

WHILES. Whilst. As amonges has been corrupted to amongst, so whiles is the original and correct form of whilst.

WHILK, e. To howl like a dog.

WHILK, e. To mutter to oneself.

WHIST, m. Silent.
"Bide whist! I hears un!"

WHITE-HERRING. A fresh herring, as distinguished from a dried one, which is called a red-herring.

WHITTLE. [Hwítel, Ang. Sax., a white mantle.] A mantle of coarse stuff formerly worn by country women.

WIDE-OF. Out of the direct road, but not far off.
"Stone is a little wide of Rye." Generally lies or lays wide of, etc.

WIDOWS-BENCH. (See Bench.)
"And that if any tenant having any land either fforrep or board die seized, his widow after his death she'd have the said lands which were her said husbands at the time of his death by the custom of the said manor as by her bench dureing her natural life, altho she marry afterward to another husband." – Bosham Manor Custom .

WILD. The Weald of Sussex is always spoken of as The Wild by the people who live in the Downs, who by the same rule call the inhabitants of the wealden district "the wild people."

WILL-LED, e. Led away or bewildered by false appearances, as a person would be who followed Will o' Wisp.

WIM. To winnow corn.

WINDROW, m. Sheaves of corn set up in a row one against the other; a thin row of new mown

The Causeway, Horsham

grass raked up lightly so as to allow the wind to pass freely through it and dry it. This grass also called leeks.

WINDROW. To put hay into windrows.

WINDSHAKEN, e. Thin, puny; weak.

"He's a poor windshaken creetur."

WINNOWING-FAG, w. A rough machine for winnowing.

WINT, e. [Windan, Ang. Sax., to turn.] Two ridges of ground which are ploughed by going to one end of the field and back again. Arable land which is harrowed twice over is said to be harrowed a wint (or a turn); if three times, a wint and a half.

WINTERPICKS. Blackthorn berries – sloes. Prunus spinosa.

WINTER-PROUD. Cold

"When you sees so many of these here winterpicks about, you may be pretty sure t'will be mid-dlin' winter proud."

WIPPANCE, w. The bar on which the traces of a horse are hooked, and by which he draws his load. Also called whippel tree, or whipple tree.

WIPPEN. Same as Wippance.

WISH. [Wesc, Ang. Sax., a washing.] A damp meadow; a marsh, or low land in a nook formed by the bend of a river or stream, and liable to be flooded

WITHY. The Willow. Salix, various species.

WRATCH or RATCH, e. [Hr'can, Ang. Sax., to reach; extend to.] To stretch.

WRIST, or RISE. [Reost, Ang. Sax., a ploughbeam.] The moveable wing (mould board) of a turn-wrist plough. (Always said with a long "i".)

WROCKLED, e. Wrinkled.

WUTS. [Corruption of Oats.]

Y

YAFFLE, e. The green woodpecker Also called Yaffingale, Galley bird and Bargeboat.

YANGER, e. [Corruption of yonder.]
"I see an old yaffle in de 'ood yanger."

YAPE, e. To gossip. (Cf. Helve an Nabble.)

YAR. Aghast; frightened.

YARBS, w. Herbs.

An old man in East Sussex said that many people set much store by the doctors, but for his part, he was one for the yarbs, and Paul Podgam was what he went by. It was not for some time that it was discovered that by Paul Podgam he meant the poly-podium fern.

YAT, m., YET, or YETE. A gate.

YEASTY, m. [Ang. Sax., yst., a storm.] Gusty; stormy.
"A little rain would do us good, but we döänt want it too oudacious yeasty."
"Though the yeasty waves Confound and swallow navigation up." – Macbeth, Act iv. sc. 1.

YEILD-IT, e. Give up.

A farmer took his team to harrow a piece of wheat, but finding it too wet he said to his carter "Come along home, we'll yeild it."

YETNER. [Git ná, Ang. Sax., not a yet.] Not nearly.
The reduplication of the negative is very common in Sussex.
"I béänt farty year old yetner."

YEO or YOWE, m. [Corruption of Ewe.] From the Ang. Sax., eowu.

YOYSTER, m. To play about roughly and noisily.

Court Lodge, Udimore

Chichester Cross

THE MUMMERS' PLAY

Dramatis Personæ

Father Christmas   A Turkish Knight
St. George   A Doctor

Father Christmas –

> *Here come I, Old Father Christmas,*
> *Christmas or not,*
> *I hope Old Father Christmas*
> *Will never be forgot.*
>
> *Make room, make room here, gallant boys,*
> *And give us room to rhyme;*
> *We've come to show activity*
> *Upon a Christmas time.*
>
> *Acting youth or acting age,*
> *The like was never acted on this stage;*
> *If you don't believe what I now say,*
> *Enter, St. George, and clear the way!*

St. George –

> *Here come I, St. George the valiant man,*
> *With naked sword and spear in hand;*
> *Who fought the dragon and brought him to the slaughter,*
> *And for this won the King of Egypt's daughter.*
> *What man or mortal dare to stand*
> *Before me with my sword in hand?*
> *I'll slay him and cut him as small as the flies,*
> *And send him to Jamaica to make mince-pies.*

Turkish Knight –
Here come I, a Turkish Knight,
In Turkish land I learned to fight;
I fought St. George with courage bold,
And if his blood's hot will make it cold

St. George –
If thou art a Turkish Knight,
Draw they sword, and let us fight.

They fight; the Turk is killed.

St. George –
Ladies and gentlemen,
You see what I've done,
I've cut this Turk down,
Like the evening sun.
Is there any doctor that can be found,
To cure this Knight of his deadly wound?

Doctor –
Here come I, a doctor,
A ten pound doctor;
I've a little bottle in my pocket
Called hokum, shokum, alicampane.
I'll touch his nose, eyes, mouth and chin
And say, "Rise, dead man," and he'll fight again.

The Turk, having been carefully examined by the doctor, is restored and immediately indicates his readiness to renew the combat.

St. George –
Here am I, St. George, with shining armour bright,
I am a famous champion, also a worthy Knight.
Seven long years in a close cave was kept,
And out of that into a prison leaped;
From out of that into a rock of stones,
There I laid down my weary bones.

Many a giant did I subdue,
And ran a fiery dragon through.
I fought the man of Tillowtree,
And still may gain the victory.
First I fought in France,
Then I fought in Spain,
And now I've come to Selmeston
To fight the Turk again.

They fight again, and St. George is again the conqueror.

St. George –
Where is the doctor that can be found
To cure the Turk of his deadly wound?

Doctor –
Hocus, pocus, alicampane,
Rise Turkish Knight to fight again.

Ladies and gentlemen, our play is ended,
Our money-box is recommended;
Copper or silver or gold if you can,
Five or six shillings will do us no harm.

See page 186 Notes on the Sussex Dialect by E. V. Lucas for a variant of the mummers' play from West Wittering.

ANGLO-SAXON NAMES IN SUSSEX

The following Anglo-Saxon words will be traced in the names of almost all the towns and villages in Sussex –

BECC. A brook. Beck. Bexhill.
BÚR. A cottage; a dwelling. Edburton.
BURH. A hill; a citadel. Burghersh; Bury; Pulborough.
BURNE. A stream; a river. Bourne. Eastbourne.
CEASTER. A camp. [From Lat. castrum.] Chester. Chichester.
COMB. A valley. [From Welsh cwm.] Combe. Balcombe.
COTE. A cot. Woodmancote; Coates.
CROFT. A small enclosed field Wivelscroft.
DAL. A valley. Dell; del. Arundel.
DENU. A valley. Den; dean. Marden; Westdean.
DÚN. A hill; a down. Don. Slindon.
EA. Water; marshy place.
Ea. Selsea; Winchelsea.
FELD. An open field; pasture; plain. Field. Heathfield.
FOLDE. A field. Fold. Slinfold.
GAT. A gate; or rather, a way; street. Gate. Rogate; Eastergate.
GRÆF. A grave; or a grove. Grove. Boxgrove.
HAM. A village; an enclosed place. Ham. Beddingham.
HOU. A hill. Hoe. Piddinghoe; Houghton.
HOLT. A grove. Wigginholt.
HURST. A wood. Nuthurst.
IG. An island. Ey. Thorney.
ING. A meadow. Angmering.
ING. Used as a patronymic; thus Wilming would signify the descendants of Wilm; whence Wilmington; Rustington, etc.
LEAG. A pasture. Ley. Earnley.

Southover Grange

MERE. A pool or lake. Mare; mere. Haremare; Tangmere.
MERSC. A marsh. Marsh. Peasmarsh.
STEDE. A place; a station. Stead; sted. Eastgrinstead; Horsted.
STÓC. A place. Stock; stoke. West Stoke.
TUN. A close; a field; a dwelling. Ton. Alciston.
WEORTHIG. A farm; an estate; a public way. Worth. Fittleworth.
WIC. A dwelling place; a village. Wick. Wick; Terwick.
WINCEL. A corner. Winchelsea. (See Wincel in Bosworth, who gives this example.)

Sussex Surnames

(Connected with Sussex words)

The following names of families, now residing in the county, are derived from or connected with Sussex words which will be found in this dictionary:–

AKEHURST. [Ang. Sax., ác, an oak, and hurst, a wood.]

ASHBURNHAM. [Ang. Sax., æsc, an ash; burne, a stream, and ham, a dwelling.]

ASHDOWN. Æsc, an ash, and dún, a hill.

ASHENDEN. Æsc, an ash, and denu, a valley.

BALKHAM. Balca, a ridge, and hám, a dwelling.

BARTON. Barton, a farmyard [Ang. Sax., bere-tún, an enclosure.]

BECK. Beck, a brook. [Ang. Sax., becc.]

BENTLEY. Bent, a tuft of grass, and ley (Ang. Sax., leag), a pasture.

BICKLEY. Beck, a brook, and ley, a pasture.

BINSTEAD. Bin and steddle, a stand.

BOURNE. A stream. [Ang. Sax., burne.]

BOSTEL. A hill path. (See Borstal.)

BRACKFIELD. Brake, a fern, and field.

BROAD. A common.

BROOKSHAW. Brook, a water-meadow, and shaw, a wood.

BURTENSHAW. Barton (bere-tún), a homestead, and shaw, a wood

BUTTERWICK. Butter, and wick, marshland.

BYTHAM. (By the ham.) Hám, a dwelling.

CALLO W. [Calo, Ang. Sax., bald] Smooth.

COCKINGE. Ing (Ang. Sax.), a son.

COMBER. Coombe, or Combe (Ang. Sax.), a valley in the downs.

COMPER. Comp (Ang. Sax.), a valley.

COPLEY. Cop, a ridge, and ley, a meadow.

CROCKER. Crock (crocca, Ang. Sax.), an earthen vessel.

CROFT. Croft (Ang. Sax.), a piece of pasture land near a house.

CROWHURST. Crow, and hurst, a wood.

DYKE. Dike (Ang. Sax., díc), a ditch.

ETHERIDGE. Ether (Ang. Sax., éther), a pliant rod, and hedge.

FELDWICK. Feld, or field, and wick, a town.

FELSTEAD. Feld, or field, and stead, a place.

GILHAM. Gill, a rivulet, and ham, a dwelling.

GRIST. Grist, a grinding; a week's allowance of flour for a family.

HASLEHURST. Hasel, and hurst, a wood

HATCH. A gate. In North of England, a heck.

HAYLEY. Hay, and ley, a meadow.

HAYWARD. A hedge-warden; an officer of the lord of the manor.

HEADLAND. A part of a field.

HEATHCOTE. Heath, and cote, or cot, a cottage.

HENTY. Hen, and tye, a common.

HIDE. [Hyd, Ang. Sax.] As much land as could be tilled with one
    plough.

HOCKHAM. [Hóh, Ang. Sax., a heel, and ham, a meadow.]

HOCKLEY. [Hoh, and leag, Ang. Sax.] Both these words mean a
    field of a certain shape. (See Hocklands.)

HOLT. [Holt, Ang. Sax., a grove.] A small plantation.

HOLTHOUSE. Holt and house.

HOOKER. (See Hockham.)

HOOKHAM. (See Hockham.)

HUCKWELL. Huck, to knock, or to spread anything about.

HURST. A wood.

HYDE. (See Hide.)

INGS. [Ing, Ang. Sax.] A common pasture.

KELK. Kilk, or charlock.

KITTLE. Kiddle, delicate; ticklish.

LADE. Part of a wagon. LANGLE~. Long and ley, a meadow.

LANGRIDGE. Long and ridge.

LANGSHAW. Long and shaw, a wood.

LANGTON. Long and ton, an enclosed place.

LEE. Leag, a meadow.

LEIGH. Leag, a meadow.

LINGHAM. Ling, a heath, and ham, an enclosure.

LONGBOTTOM. Long, and bottom, a valley in the downs (the

Old Shoreham Church

long valley).

LONGHURST. The long wood.

LONGLEY. The long meadow. (See Langley.)

MEERES. Mere, a marsh.

NAPPER. Napery, linen. (Knapper?)

PEART. Lively.

PECK. An agricultural implement.

PELLING. Pell, a pool, and ing, a pasture.

RAVENSCROFT. Raven, and croft, a field.

REEVE. An officer of the manor.

SHAW. A wood.

STEAD. An enclosed place.

SOUTHERDEN. The south valley.

WENHAM. Wen, or wain, a wagon, and ham, an enclosure. The wagon-house.

WENMAN. The wagon-man.

WHEATCROFT. The wheat field.

WOODWARD. An officer of the manor; a wood-warden.

WYNDHAM. Wynd, a path up a hill, and ham.

SUSSEX SURNAMES

BOURNE. [Burne, Ang. Sax.] A stream.

Boorne	Bourne	Bourner	Michelbourne

BROOK. A stream; a water-meadow.

Brook	Brookfield	Colbrook
Broaks	Brookshaw	

COMP. A valley.

Comper	Compton.

COOMBE, or COMBE. A hollow in the downs.

Combe	Balcombe	Farncomb	Titcombe
Comber	Dunscombe	Farncombe	Whitcombe
Anscombe	Ellcome	Lipscombe	Witcomb

CROFT. [AnG. Sax.] A small enclosed field near a house.

Croft	Horsecroft	Pycroft	Tredcroft
Crofts	Longcroft	Ravenscroft	Wheatcroft

DEN, or DENE. A valley.

Barnden	Farenden	Holden	Rigden
Blagden	Fogden	Norden	Standen
Blunden	Gosden	Ockenden	Southerden
Brigden	Hebden	Pagden	Wickenden
Cobden	Hepden	Pattenden	Wisden
Cruttenden	Hobden	Ramsden	Witherden

HAM. (1) A hamlet; (2) an enclosed place.

Balkham	Grabham	Markham	Stopham
Barham	Gresham	Mepham	Southam
Bellingham	Grinham	Milham	Tatham
Benham	Hardham	Needham	Wenham
Bromham	Higham	Oldham	Wapham
Clapham	Hockham	Oxenham	Wickham
Cobham	Hookham	Paxkham	Witham
Coldham	Kingham	Pelham	Woodham

| Cosham | Langham | Sandham | Woodhams |
| Gilham | Lingham | Stoneham | Wyndham |

HURST. [Ang. Sax.] A wood.

Hurst	Crowhurst	Luckhurst	Songhurst
Brinkhurst	Folkhurst	Medhurst	Ticehurst
Broadhurst	Haslehurst	Pankhurst	Wilmshurst
	Longhurst	Staplehurst	

LEY. [Ang. Sax.. Ieag.] A pastureland.

Ley	Ernley	Hoadley	Morley
Bayley	Graveley	Hockley	Notley
Bentley	Handley	Huntley	Nutley
Bletchley	Hawley	Langley	Oakley
Burley	Hayley	Lee	Pelley
Cawley	Helmsley	Leigh	Popley
Copley	Hemsley	Longley	Ripley
Cowley	Henley	Lutley	Stapley
Crutchley	Hickley	Medley	Wheatley
			Worsley

SHAW. A small wood on a hill side.

Shaw	Brookshaw	Buttonshaw	Langshaw
Bagshaw	Burstenshaw	Crawshaw	Oldershaw
	Burtenshaw	Henshaw	

STEAD. [Ang. Sax.] A place.

Stead	Grinstead	Hempsted	Polsted
Felstead	Halstead	Isted	Steadman
	Halsted	Maxted	

WICK. [Ang. Sax.] A town.

Wicks	Feldwick	Markwick	Wickerson
Butterwick	Gratwick	Padwick	Wickham
Chadwick	Hardwick	Rudwick	Wickenden
	Madgwick	Strudwick	

162

A Miscellany from E. V. Lucas

A Glimpse of the Old Sussex Field Routine

This had not greatly changed in the remote districts and was given to Mr. Gordon about 1875 by an aged labourer. This was the day:–

"Out in morning at four o'clock. Mouthful of bread and cheese and pint of ale. Then off to the harvest field. Rippin and moen [reaping and mowing] till eight. Then morning brakfast and small beer. Brakfast – a piece of fat pork as thick as your hat [a broad-brimmed wideawake] is wide. Then work till ten o'clock: then a mouthful of bread and cheese and a pint of strong beer ['farnooner,' i.G., forenooner; 'farnooner's-lunch,' we called it]. Work till twelve. Then at dinner in the farm-house; sometimes a leg of mutton, sometimes a piece of ham and plum pudding. Then work till five, then a *nunch* and a quart of ale. Nunch was cheese, 'twas skimmed cheese though. Then work till sunset, then home and have supper and a pint of ale. I never knew a man drunk in the harvest field in my life. Could drink six quarts, and believe that a man might drink two gallons in a day. All of us were in the house [*i.e.*, the usual hired servants, and those specially engaged for the harvest]: the yearly servants used to go with the monthly ones.

"There were two thrashers, and the head thrasher used always to go before the reapers. A man could cut according to the goodness of the job, half-an-acre a day. The terms of wages were £3 10s. to 50s. for the month.

"When the hay was in cock or the wheat in shock, then the Titheman come; you didn't dare take up a field without you let him know. If the Titheman didn't come at the time, you tithed yourself. He marked his sheaves with a bough or bush. You couldn't get over the Titheman. If you began at a hedge and made the tenth cock smaller than the rest, the Titheman might begin in the middle

Cottages at Slinfold

just where he liked. The Titheman at Harting, old John Blackmore, lived at Mundy's [South Harting Street]. His grandson is blacksmith at Harting now. All the tithing was quiet. You didn't dare even set your eggs till the Titheman had been and ta'en his tithe. The usual day's work was from 7 to 5."

Bramber

Proverbs

A local proverb says that if you eat winkles in March it is as good as a dose of medicine; which reminds me that Sussex has many wise sayings of its own. Here is a piece of Sussex counsel in connection with the roaring month:–

> If from fleas you would be free,
> On the first of March let all your windows closed be.

I quote two other rhymes:–

> If you would wish your bees to thrive
> Gold must be paid for every hive;
> For when they're bought with other money
> There will be neither swarm nor honey.

> The first butterfly you see,
> Cut off his head across your knee,
> Bury the head under a stone
> And a lot of money will be your own.

On Whit Sunday the devout Sussex man eats roast veal and gooseberry pudding. A Sussex child born on Sunday can neither be hanged nor drowned.

A DRAGON, A HEADLESS HORSEMAN AND NIGHTINGALES

I have seen grass snakes in plenty in St. Leonard's Forest, and was once there with a botanist who, the day being fine, killed a particularly beautiful one; but the Forest is no longer famous, as once it was, for really alarming reptiles. The year 1614 was the time. A rambler in the neighbourhood, in August of that year, ran the risk of meeting something worth running away from; just as John Steel, Christopher Holder, and a widow woman did. Their story may be read in the Harleian Miscellany. *True and Wonderful* is the title of the narrative, *A Discourse relating a strange and monstrous Serpent (or Dragon) lately discovered, and yet living, to the great Annoyance and divers Slaughters both of Men and Cattell, by his strong and violent Poyson: In Sussex, two Miles from Horsam, in a Woode called St. Leonards Forrest, and thirtie Miles from London, this present Month of August, 1614. With the true Generation of Serpents.* The discourse runs thus:—

"In Sussex, there is a pretty market-towne, called Horsam, neare unto it a forrest, called St. Leonard's Forrest, and there, in a vast and unfrequented place, heathie, vaultie, full of unwholesome shades, and over-growne hollowes, where this serpent is thought to be bred; but, wheresoever bred, certaine and too true it is, that there it yet lives. Within three or four miles compasse, are its usual haunts, oftentimes at a place called Faygate, and it hath been seene within halfe a mile of Horsam; a wonder, no doubt, most terrible and noisome to the inhabitants thereabouts. There is always in his tracke or path left a glutinous and slimie matter (as by a small similitude we may perceive in a snaile's) which is very corrupt and offensive to the scent; insomuch that they perceive the air to be putrified withall, which must needes be very dangerous. For though the corruption of it cannot strike the outward part of a man, unless heated into his blood; yet by receiving it in at any of our breathing organs (the mouth or nose) it is by authoritie of all authors, writing in that kinde, mortall and deadlie, as one thus saith:

"Noxia serpentum est admixto sanguine pestis. – LUCAN.

"This serpent (or dragon, as some call it) is reputed to be nine feete, or rather more, in length, and shaped almost in the forme of an axeltree of a cart; a quantitie of thickness in the middest, and somewhat smaller at both endes. The former part, which he shootes forth as a necke, is supposed to be an elle long; with a white ring, as it were, of scales about it. The scales along his backe seem to be blackish, and so much as is discovered under his bellie, appeareth to be red; for I speak of no nearer description than of a reasonable ocular distance. For coming too neare it, hath already beene too dearely payd for, as you shall heare hereafter.

"It is likewise discovered to have large feete, but the eye may be there deceived; for some suppose that serpents have no feete, but glide upon certain ribbes and scales, which both defend them from the upper part of their throat unto the lower part of their bellie, and also cause them to move much the faster. For so this doth, and rids way (as we call it) as fast as a man can run. He is of countenance very proud, and at the sight or hearing of men or cattel, will raise his necke upright, and seem to listen and looke about, with great arrogancy. There are likewise on either side of him discovered, two great bunches so big as a large foote-ball, and (as some thinke) will in time grow to wings; but God, I hope, will (to defend the poor people in the neighbourhood) that he shall be destroyed before he grow so fledge.

"He will cast his venome about four rodde from him, as by woe-full experience it was proved on the bodies of a man and a woman comming that way, who afterwards were found dead, being poysoned and very much swelled, but not prayed upon. Likewise a man going to chase it, and as he imagined, to destroy it with two mastive dogs, as yet not knowing the great danger of it, his dogs were both killed, and he himselfe g]ad to returne with hast to preserve his own life. Let this is to be noted, that the dogs were not prayed upon, but slaine and left whole: for his food is thought to be, for the most part, in a conie-warren, which he much frequents; and it is found much scanted and impaired in the encrease it had woont to afford.

"These persons, whose names are hereunder printed, have seene this serpent, beside divers others, as thc carrier of Horsam, who lieth at the White Horse in Southwarke, and who can certifie the truth of all that has been here related.

John Steele.
Christopllcr Holder.
And a Widow Woman dwelling nere Faygate."

It would be very interesting to know what John Steele, Christopher Holder, and the widow woman really saw. Such a story must have had a basis of some kind. A printed narrative such as this would hardly have proceeded from a clear sky.

St. Leonard's Forest has another familiar; for there the headless horseman rides, not on his own horse, but on yours, seated on the crupper with his ghostly arms encircling your waist. His name is Powlett, but I know no more, except that his presence is an additional reason why one should explore the forest on foot.

Sussex, especially near the coast, is naturally a good nightingale country. Many of the birds, pausing there after their long journey at the end of April, do not fly farther, but make their home where they first alight. I know of one meadow and copse under the north escarpment of the Downs where three nightingales singing in rivalry in a triangle (the perfect condition) can be counted upon in May, by night, and often by day too, as surely as the rising and setting of the sun. But in St. Leonard's Forest the nightingale never sings. American visitors who, as Mr. John Burroughs once did, come to England in the spring to hear the nightingale, must remember this.

On the Ouse above Lewes

BIRD-CATCHING

Of old the best wheatear country was above Rottingdean; but the South Down shepherds no longer have the wheatear money that used to add so appreciably to their wages in the summer months. A combination of circumstances has brought about this loss. One is the decrease in wheatears, another the protection of the bird by law, and a third the refusal of the farmers to allow their men any longer to neglect the flocks by setting and tending snares. But in the seventeenth, eighteenth and early part of the nineteenth centuries, wheatears were taken on the Downs in enormous quantities and formed a part of every south county banquet in their season. People visited Brighton solely to eat them, as they now go to Greenwich for whitebait and to Colchester for oysters.

This is how Fuller describes the little creature in the "Worthies"– *Wheatears* is a bird peculiar to this County, hardly found out of it. It is so called, because fattest when Wheat is ripe, whereon it feeds; being no bigger than a Lark, which it equalleth in the *fineness* of the flesh, far exceedeth in the *fatness* thereof. The worst is, that being onely seasonable in the heat of summer, and naturally larded with lumps of fat, it is soon subject to corrupt, so that (though abounding within *fourty* miles) *London Poulterers* have no mind to meddle with them, which no care in carriage can keep from Putrefaction. That *Palate-man* shall pass in silence, who, being seriously demanded his judgment concerning the abilities of a great *Lord*, concluded him a man of very weak parts, ' *because once he saw him, at* a great Feast, *feed on* CHICKENS *when there were* WHEAT EARS *on the table.'* I will adde no more in praise of this *Bird*, for fear some *female Reader* may fall in *longing* for it, and unhappily be disappointed of her desire." A contemporary of Fuller, John Taylor, thus unscientifically dismisses the wheatear in one of his doggerel narratives:—

Six weeks or thereabouts they are catch'd there,
And are well-nigh 11 months God knows where.

As a matter of fact, the winter home of the wheatear is Africa.

The capture of wheatears – mostly illegally by nets – still continues in a very small way to meet a languid demand, but the Sussex ortolan, as the little bird was sometimes called, has passed from the bill of fare. Wheatears (which, despite Fuller, have no connection with ears of wheat, the word signifying white tail) still abound, skimming over the turf in little groups; but they ro longer fly towards the dinner table. The best and most interesting description that I know of the old manner of taking them, is to be found in Mr. W. H. Hudson's *Nature in Downland*. The season began in July, when the little fat birds rest on the Downs on their way from Scotland and northern England to their winter home, and lasted through September. In July, says Mr. Hudson, the "Shepherds made their 'coops,' as their traps were called – a **T**-shaped trench about fourteen inches long, over which the two long narrow sods cut neatly out of the turf were adjusted, grass downwards. A small opening was left at the end for ingress, and there was room in the passage for the bird to pass through towards the chinks of light coming from the two ends of the cross passage. At the inner end of the passage a horse-hair springe was set, by which the bird was caught by the neck as it passed in, but the noose did not as a rule strangle the bird. On some of the high downs near the coast, notably at Beachy Head; at Birling Gap, at Seaford, and in the neighbourhood of Rottingdean, the shepherds made so many coops, placed at small distances apart, that the Downs in some places looked as if they had been ploughed. In September, when the season was over, the sods were carefully put back, roots down, in the places, and the smooth green surface was restored to the hills."

On bright clear days few birds would be caught, but in showery weather the traps would all be full; this is because when the sun is obscured wheatears are afraid and take refuge under stones or in whatever hole may offer. The price of each wheatear was a penny, and it was the custom of the persons in the neighbourhood who wanted then for dinner to visit the traps, take out the birds and leave the money in their place. The shepherd on returning would collect his gains and reset the traps. Near Brighton, however, most of the shepherds caught only for dealers; and one firm, until some twenty years ago, maintained the practice of giving an annual supper at the end of the season, at which the shepherds would be paid in the mass for their spoil.

An old shepherd, who had been for years on Westside Farm near Brighton, spoke thus, in 1882, as Mr. Borrer relates in his *Birds of Sussex*:– "The most I ever caught in one day was thirteen dozen, but we thought it a good day if we caught three or four dozen. We sold them to a poulterer at Brighton, who took all we could catch in a season at 18d. a dozen. From what I have heard from old shepherds, it cannot be doubted that they were caught in much greater numbers a century ago than of late. I have heard them speak of an immense number being taken in one day by a shepherd at East Dean, near Beachy Head. I think they said he took nearly a hundred dozen, so many that they could not thread them on crow-quills in the usual manner, but he took off his round frock and made a sack of it to put them into, and his wife did the same with her petticoat. This must have happened when there was a great flight. Their numbers now are so decreased that some shephcrds do not set up any coops, as it does not pay for the trouble."

Although wheatears are no longer caught, the Brighton bird catcher is a very busy man. Goldfinches fall in extraordinary plenty to his nets. A bird-catcher told Mr. Borrer that he once caught eleven dozen of them at one haul, and in I860 the annual take at Worthing was 1.154 dozen. Larks are also caught in great numbers, also with nets, the old system still practised in France, of luring them with glasses, having become obsolete. Knox has an interesting description of the lark-glass and its uses:– "A piece of wood about a foot and a half long, four inches deep, and three inches wide, is planed off on two sides so as to resemble the roof of a well-known toy, yclept a Noah's ark, but more than twice as long. In the sloping sides are set several bits of looking-glass. A long iron spindle, the lower end of which is sharp and fixed in the ground, passes freely through the centre; on this the instrument turns, and even spins rapidly when a string has been attached and is pulled by the performer, who generally stands at a distance of fifteen or twenty yards from the decoy. The reflection of the sun's rays from these little revolving mirrors seems to possess a mysterious attraction for the larks, for they descend in great numbers from a considcrable height in the air, hover over the spot, and suffer themselves to be shot at repeatedly without attempting to leave the field or to continue their course."

A SMUGGLER'S GRAVE

On the way to Brighton from the Plough one passes through Patcham, a dusty village that for many years has seen too many bicycles, and now is in the way of seeing too many motor cars. In the churchyard is, or was, a tomb bearing the following inscription, which may be quoted both as a reminder of the more stirring experiences to which the Patcham people were subject a hundred years ago, and also as an example of the truth which is only half a truth:

Sacred to the memory of Daniel Scales, who was unfortunately shot on Thursday Evening, Nov. 7, 1796.

Alas! swift flew the fatal lead
Which pierced through the young man's head,
He instant fell, resigned his breath,
And closed his languid eyes in death.
All ye who do this stone draw near,
Oh! pray let fall the pitying tear.
From the sad instance may we all
Prepare to meet Jehovah's call.

The facts of the case bear some likeness to the death of Mr. Bardell and Serjeant Buzfuz's reference to that catastrophe. Daniel Scales was a desperate smuggler who, when the fatal lead pierced him, was heavily laden with booty. He was shot through the head only as a means of preventing a similar fate befalling his slayer.

RECIPES AND RECEIPTS

I must quote a prescription from the diary (Richard Stapley of Hickstead Place):– "To cure the hoopingcough:– get 3 field mice, flaw them, draw them, and roast one of them, and let the party afflicted eat it; dry the other two in the oven until they crumble to a powder, and put a little of this powder in what the patient drinks at night and in the morning." Mice played, and still play in remote districts, a large part in the rural pharmacopeia. A Sussex doctor once told me that he had directed the mother of a boy at Portslade to put some ice in a bag and tie it on the boy's forehead. When, the next day, the doctor asked after his patient, the mother replied briskly :– "Oh, Tommy's better, but the mice are dead."

The Stapley family ate an oatmeal pudding made in the following manner:–

> Of oats decorticated take two pound,
> And of new milk enough the same to dround;
> Of raisins of the sun, ston'd, ounces eight;
> Of currants, cleanly picked, an equal weight;
> Of suet, finely sliced, an ounce at least:
> And six eggs newly taken from the nest
> Season this mixture well with salt and spice;
> Twill make a pudding far exceeding nice;
> And you may safely feed on it like farmers.
> For the receipt is learned Dr. Harmer's.

Leonard Mascall of Plumpton Place wrote and translated several books, among them a treatise on the orchard by a monk of the Abbey of St. Vincent in France: *A Book of the Arte of and Manner howe to plant and graffe all sortes of trees, howe to set stones, and sowe Pepines to make wylde trees to graffe on*, 1572. I take a few passages from a later edition of this work:

TO COLOUR APPLES

To have coloured Apples with what colour ye shall think good ye shall bore or slope a hole with an Auger in the biggest part of the body of the tree, unto the midst thereof, or there abouts, and then look what colour ye will have them of. First ye shall take water and

Steyning Church

mingle your colour there with, then stop it up again with a short pin made of the same wood or tree, then wax it round about. Ye may mingle with the said colour what spice ye list, to make them taste thereafter. Thus may ye change the colour and taste of any Apple... This must be done before the Spring do come...

TO MAKE APPLES FALL FROM THE TREE
If ye put fiery coles under an Apple tree, and then cast off the powder of Brimstone therein, and the fume thereof ascend up, and touch an Apple that is wet, that Apple shall fall incontinant.

TO DESTROY PISMERS OR ANTS ABOUT A TREE
Ye shall take of the saw-dust of Oke-wood oney, and straw that al about the tree root, and the next raine that doth come, all the Pismiers or Ants shall die there. For Earewigges, shooes stopt with hay, and hanged on the tree one night, they come all in.

FOR TO HAVE RATH MEDLERS TWO MONTHS BEFORE OTHERS
For to have Medlars two months sooner than others and the one shall be better far than the other, ye shall graffe them upon a gooseberry tree, and also a franke mulberry tree, and before ye do graffe them, ye shall wet them in hay, and then graffe them.

SUSSEX NAMES

Some of the oddest of the composite pietistic names that broke out over England during the Puritan revolution are to be found in Sussex registers. In 1632, Master Performe-thy-vowes Seers of Maresfield married Thomasine Edwards. His full name was too much for the village, and four years later is found an entry recording the burial of "Vowes Seers" pure and simple. The searcher of parish registers from whose articles in the *Sussex Daily News* I have already quoted, has also found that Heathfield had many Puritan names, among them "Replenished," which was given to the daughter of Robert Pryor in 1600. There was also a Heathfield damsel known as "More-Fruits." Mr. Lower prints the following names from a Sussex jury list in the seventeenth century: Redeemed Compton of Battel, Stand-fast-on-high Stringer of Crowhurst, Weep-not Billing of Lewes, Called Lower of Warbleton, Elected Mitchell of Heathfield, Renewed Wisberry of Hailsham, Fly-fornication Richardson of Waldron, The-Peace-of-God Knight of Burwash, Fight-the-good-fight of faith White of Ewhurst, and Kill-sin Pemble of Withyham. Also a Master More-Fruits Fowler of East Hoathly, for it seems that in such names there was no sex. Among the curious Sussex surnames found by the student of the county archives who is quoted above are the following:–

Pitchfork	Sweetnarnc	Lies
Devil	Slybody	Hogsflesh
Leper	Fidge	Backfield
Handshut	Beatup	Breathing
Juglery	Rougehead	Whiskey
Hollowbone	Punch	Wildgoose
Stillborne	Padge	Ann

In losing your way in the Alfriston neighbourhood do not ask the passer-by for Selmeston, but for Simson; for Selmeston, pronounced as spelt, does not exist. Sussex men are curiously intolerant of the phonetics of orthography. Brighthelmstone was called Brighton from the first, although only in the last century was the spelling modified to agree with the sound. Chalvington (the name of a village north of Selmeston) is a pretty word, but Sussex declines to call it other than Chawton. Firle becomes Furrel; Lewes

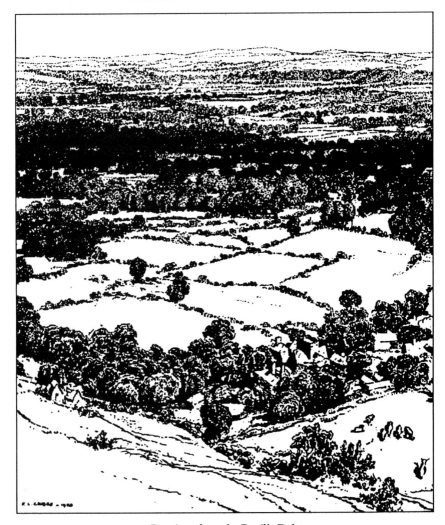

Poynings from the Devil's Dyke

is almost Lose, but not quite; Heathfield is Hefful. It is characteristic of a Sussex man that he always knows best; though all the masters of all the colleges should assemble about him and speak reasoningly of Selmeston he would leave the congress as incorrigible and self-satisfied a Simsonian as ever.

HARVEST HOME

One does not think naturally of old Sussex customs in connection with this town (Hastings), so thoroughly urban as it now is and so largely populated by visitors, but I find in the Sussex Archaeological Collections the following interesting account, by a Hastings alderman, of an old harvest ceremony in the neighbourhood:– "At the head of the table one of the men occupied the position of chairman; in front of him stood a pail – clean as wooden staves and iron hoops could be made by human labour. At his right sat four or five men who led the singing, grave as judges were they; indeed, the appearance of the whole assembly was one of the greatest solemnity, except for a moment or two when some unlucky wight failed to 'turn the cup over,' and was compelled to undergo the penalty in that case made and provided. This done, all went on as solemnly as before.

"The ceremony, if I may call it so, was this: The leader, or chairman, standing behind the pail with a tall horn cup in his hand, filled it with beer from the pail. The man next to him on the left stood up, and holding a hat with both hands by the brim, crown upwards, received the cup from the chairman, on the crown of the hat, not touching it with either hand. He then lifted the cup to his lips by raising the hat, and slowly drank off the contents. As soon as he began to drink, the chorus struck up this chant:

I"ve bin to Plymouth and I've bin to Dover.
I have bin rambling, boys, all the wurld over –
  Over and over and over and over,
Drink up yur liquor and turn yur Cup over;
  Over and over and over and over,
The liquor's drink'd up and the cup is turned over.

"The man drinking was expected to time his draught so as to empty his cup at the end of the fourth line of the chant; he was then to return the hat to the perpendicular, still holding the hat by the brim, then to throw the cup into the air, and reversing the hat, to catch the cup in it as it fell. If he failed to perform this operation, the fellow workmen who were closely watching him, made an important alteration in the last line of their chant, which in that case ran thus:

The liquor's drink'd up and the cup *aint* turned over.

"The cup was then refilled and the unfortunate drinker was

Udimore Church

compelled to go through the same ceremony again. Every one at the table took the cup and 'turned it over' in succession, the chief shepherd keeping the pail constantly supplied with beer. The parlour guests were of course invited to turn the cup over with the guests of the kitchen, and went through the ordeal with more or less of success. For my own part, I confess that I failed to catch the cup in the hat at the first trial and had to try again; the chairman, however, mercifully gave me only a small quantity of beer the second time."

THE SUSSEX DIALECT

The body of the Sussex dialect is derived from the Saxon. Its accessories can be traced to the Celts, to the Norse – thus *rape*, a division of the county, is probably an adaptation of the Icelandic *hreppr* – and to the French, some hundreds of Huguenots having fled to our shores after the Edict of Nantes. The Hastings fishermen, for example, often say *boco* for plenty, and *frap* to strike; while in the Rye neighbourhood, where the Huguenots were strongest, such words as *dishabil* meaning untidy, undressed, and *peter grievous* (from petit-grief) meaning fretful, are still used.

But Saxon words are, of course, considerably more common. You meet them at every turn. A Sussex auctioneer's list that lies before me – a catalogue of live and dead farming stock to be sold at a homestead under the South Downs – is full of them. So blunt and sturdy they are, these ancient primitive terms of the soil: "Lot 1. Pitch prong, two half-pitch prongs, two 4-speen spuds, and a road hoe. Lot 5. Five short prongs, flint spud, dung drag, two turnip pecks, and two shovels. Lot 9. Six hay rakes, two scythes and sneaths, cross-cut saw, and a sheep hook. Lot 39. Corn chest, open tub, milking stool, and hog form. Lot 43. Bushel measure, shaul and strike. Lot 100. Rick borer. Lot 143. Eight knaves and seven felloes. Lot 148. Six dirt boards and pair of wood hames. Lot 152. Wheelwright's sampson. Lot 174. Set of thill harness. Lot 201. Three plough bolts, three tween sticks. Lot 204. Sundry harness and whippances. Lot 208. Tickle plough. Lot 222. Iron turnwrist [pronounced turn-riced] plough. Lot 242. 9-time scarifier. Lot 25I. Clod crusher. Lot 252. Hay tedder." From another catalogue more ram=alogues, these abrupt and active little words might be called, butt at one. As "Lot 4. Flint spud, two drain scoops, bull lead and five dibbles. Lot. 10. Dung rake and dung devil. Lot 11. Four juts and a zinc skip." Farm labourers are men of little speech, and it is often needful that voices should carry far. Hence this crisp and forcible reticence. The vocabulary of the country-side undergoes few changes; and the noises to-day made by the ox-herd who urges his black and smoking team along the hill-side are precisely those that Piers Plowman himself would have used.

Another survival may be noticed in objurgation. A Sussex man swearing by Job, as he often does, is not calling in the aid of the patient sufferer of Uz, but Jobe, the Anglo-Saxon Jupiter.

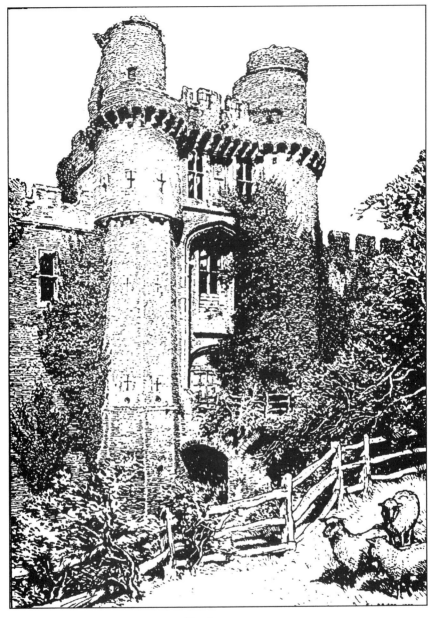

Hurstmonceux

Roughly speaking, Sussex has little or no dialect absolutely its own; for the country speech of the west is practically that also of Hampshire, and of the east, that of Kent. The dividing line between east and west, Mr. Cripps of Steyning tells me, is the Adur, once an estuary of the sea rather than the stream it now is, running far inland and separating the two Sussexes with its estranging wave.

In Mr. Coker Egerton's *Sussex Folk and Sussex Ways* is an amusing example of gender in Sussex. The sun, by the way, is always she or her to the Sussex peasant, as to the German savant; but it is not the only unexpected feminine in the county. Mr. Egerton gives a conversation in a village school, in which the master bids Tommy blow his nose. A little later he returns, and asks Tommy why he has not done so. "Please, sir, I did blow her, but her wouldn't bide blowed."

In his dictionary Mr. Parish has perhaps made the Sussex labourer a thought too epigrammatic: a natural tendency in the illustrations to such a work. The following narrative of adventure from the lips of a South Down shepherd, which is communicated to me by my friend, Mr. C. E. Clayton, of Holmbush, is nearer the normal loquacity of the type:– " I mind one day I'd been to buy some lambs, and coming home in the dark over the bostal, I gets to a field, and I knows there was a geat, and I kep' beating the hedge with my stick to find the geat, and at last I found 'en, and I goos to get over 'en, and 'twas one of these here gurt ponds full of foul water I'd mistook for the geat, and so in I went, all over my head, and I tumbles out again middlin' sharp, and I slips, 'cause 'twas so slubby, and in I goos again, and I do think I should ha' been drownded if it warn't for my stick, and I was that froughtened, and there were some bullocks close by, and I froughtened them splashing about and they began to run round, and that froughtened me; and there – well, I was all wet through and grabby, and when I got home I looked like one of these here water-cress men. But I kep' my pipe in my mouth all the time. I didn't lose 'en."

The late Mr. F. E. Sawyer, another student of Sussex dialect, has remarked on the similarity between Sussex provincialisms and many words which we are accustomed to think peculiarly American. One cause may be the two hundred Sussex colonists taken over by William Penn, who, as we have seen, was at one time

Amberley Castle

Squire of Warminghurst. "In recent years we have gathered from the works of American comic writers and others many words which at first have been termed 'vulgar Americanisms,' but which, on closer examination, have proved to be good old Anglo-Saxon and other terms which had dropped out of notice amongst us, but were retained in the *New* World! Take, for instance, two 'Southern words,' (probably Sussex) quoted by Ray (1674). *Squirm* :— Artemus Ward describes 'Brother Uriah,' of 'the Shakers,' as '*squirming* liked a speared eel,' and, curiously enough, Ray gives 'To *squirm*, to move nimbly about after the manner of an eel. It is spoken of eel.' Another word is 'sass' (for sauce), also quoted by Artemus Ward... Mrs. Phcebe Earl Gibbons (an American lady), in a clever and instructive article in *Harper's Magazine* on 'English Farmers' (but, in fact, describing the agriculture, &c., of Sussex in a very interesting way), considers that the peculiarities of the present Sussex dialect resemble those of New England more than of Pennsylvania. She mentions as Sussex phrases used in New England – 'You hadn't ought to do it,' and 'You shouldn't ought'; 'Be you'? for 'Are you'? 'I see him,' for 'I saw.' 'You have a *crock* on your nose,' for a smut; *nuther* for neither; *passel* for parcel, and a *pucker* for a fuss. In addition she observes that Sussex people speak of ' the *fall*' for autumn and 'guess' and 'reckon' like genuine Yankees." So far Mr. Sawyer. Sussex people also, I might add, "disremember," as Huck Finn used to do.

The Song of Solomon in Sussex Dialect

I should like to quote a few verses from the Sussex version of the "Song of Solomon," which Mr. Lower prepared for Prince Lucien Buonaparte some forty years ago. The experiment was extended to other southern and western dialects, the collection making a little book of curious charm and homeliness. Here is the fourth chapter:–

I. Lookee, you be purty, my love, lookee, you be purty. You've got dove's eyes adin yer locks; yer hair is like a flock of goäts dat appear from Mount Gilead.

2. Yer teeth be lik a flock of ship just shared, dat come up from de ship-wash; every one of em bears tweens, an nare a one among em is barren.

3. Yer lips be lik a thread of scarlet, an yer speech is comely; yer temples be lik a bit of a pomgranate adin yer locks.

4. Yer nick is lik de tower of Daöved, built for an armoury, what dey heng a thousan bucklers on, all shields of mighty men.

5. Yer two brestes be lik two young roes, what be tweens, dat feed among de lilies.

6. Till de dee break, an der shadders goo away, I'll git me to de mountain of myrrh, and to de hill of frankincense.

7. You be hem purty, my love; der aunt a spot in ye.

8. Come along wud me from Lebanon, my spouse, wud me from Lebanon: look from de top of Amana, from de top of Shenir an Hermon, from de lions' dens, from de mountain of de leopards.

9. Ye've stole away my heart, my sister, my spouse. Ye've stole away my heart wud one of yer eyes, wud one chain of yer nick.

10. How fair is yer love, my sister, my spouse! how much better is yer love dan wine! an de smell of yer intments dan all spices.

11. Yer lips, O my spouse, drap lik de honeycomb; dere's honey an melk under yer tongue; an de smell of yer garments is lik de smell of Lebanon.

12. A fenced garn is my sister, my spouse, a spring shet up, a fountain sealed.

13. Yer plants be an archard of pomegranates wud pleasant fruits, camphire an spikenard.

14. Spikenard an saffron, calamus an cinnamon, wud all trees of frankincense, myrrh, an allers, wud all de best of spices.

15. A fountain of garns, a well of livin waters, an straims from

Cuckfield Church

Lebanon.

16. Wake, O north win, an come, ye south; blow upon my garn, dat de spices of it may flow out. Let my beloved come into his garn, an ait his pleasant fruits.

THE WEST WITTERING MUMMERS' PLAY

At West Wittering in the Manhood Peninsula, a little village on which the sea has hostile designs, is still performed at Christmas a time-honoured play the actors of which are half a dozen boys or men known as the Tipteers. Their words are not written, but are transmitted orally from one generation of players to another. Mr. J. I. C. Boger, however, has taken them down. The subject once again, as in some of the Hardham mural paintings, is the life of St. George, here called King George; and the play has the same relation to drama that the Hardham frescoes have to a picture. I quote a little:–

Third man – Noble Captain:

> *In comes I, the Noble Captain,*
> *Just lately come from France;*
> *With my broad sword and jolly Turk [dirk]*
> *I will make King George dance.*

Fourth Man – King George [i.e., Saint George]:

> *In comes I, King George,*
> *That man of courage bold,*
> *With my broad sword and sphere [spear]*
> *I have won ten tons of gold.*
> *I fought the fiery Dragon*
> *And brought it to great slaughter,*
> *And by that means I wish to win*
> *The King of Egypt's daughter.*
> *Neither unto thee will I bow nor bend.*
> *Stand off! stand off!*
> *I will not take you to be my friend.*

Noble Captain:

> *Why, sir, why, have I done you any kind of wrong?*

King George:

> *Yes, you saucy man, so get you gone.*

Noble Captain: .

> *You saucy nun, you draw my name,*

You ought to be stabb'd, you saucy man.

King George:

> *Stab or stabs, the least is my fear;*
> *Point me the place*
> *And I will meet you there.*

Noble Captain:

> *The place I 'point is on the ground*
> *And there I will lay your body down*
> *Across the water at the hour of five.*

King George:

> *Done, sir, done ! I will meet you there,*
> *If I am alive I will cut you, I will slay you,*
> *All for to let you know that I am King George over Great Britain O !*

FIGHT: [King George wounds the Noble Captain.]

Until the close is almost reached the West Wittering Tipteers preserve the illusion of mediaeval mummery. But the concluding song transports us to the sentiment of the modern music hall. Its chorus runs, with some callousness:–

> *"We never miss a mother till she's gone,*
> *Her portrait's all we have to gaze upon,*
> *We can fancy see her there,*
> *Sitting in an old armchair;*
> *We never miss a mother till she's gone."*

THE SMUGGLER

With Mr. Lower's assistance, I add a few words on the difficulties that confronted the London revenue officers in the Sussex humour. To be confounded by too swift a horse or too agile a "runner" was all in the night's work; but to be hoodwinked and bamboozled by the deliberate stealthy southern fun must have been eternally galling. The Sussex joker grinds slowly and exceeding small; but the flour is his. "There was Nick Cossum the blacksmith [the words are a shepherd's, talking to Mr. Lower]; he was a sad plague to them. Once he made an exciseman run several miles after him, to take away a keg of *yeast* he was a-carrying to Ditchling! Another

Pulborough Church

The Rother at Fittleworth

time as he was a-going up New Bostall, an exciseman, who knew him of old, saw him a-carrying a tub of hollands. So he says, says he, 'Master Cossum, I must have that tub of yours, I reckon!' 'Worse luck, I suppose you must,' says Nick in a civil way, 'though it's rather again' the grain to be robbed like this; but, however, I am a-going your road, and we can walk together – there's no law again' that I expect.' 'Oh, certainly not,' says the other, taking of the tub upon his shoulders. So they chatted along quite friendly and *chucker* like till they came to a cross road, and Nick wished the excise man good bye. After Nick had got a little way, he turned round all of a sudden and called out: 'Oh, there's one thing I forgot; here's a little bit o' paper that belongs to the keg.' 'Paper,' says the exciseman, 'why, that's a permit, says he; 'why didn't you show me that when I took the hollands?' 'Oh,' says Nick, as saucy as Hinds, 'why, if I had done that,' says he, 'you wouldn't a carried my tub for me all this way, would you?' "

CHIDDINGLY HOT-POT

Said to have been created by Edward Shoosmith of Street Chiddingly, in 1917.

450g (1 Ib.) onions, skinned and chopped
1 head celery, wiped and chopped
1OOg (4 oz.) black olives, stoned and roughly chopped
900g (2 Ib.) braising steak, cut up
90ml (6 tbsp) vinegar
8 whole allspice
8 cloves
4 blades mace
freshly milled black pepper
salt 900g
(2 Ib.) potatoes, peeled and thinly sliced
600ml (1 pint) beef stock
Serves 6-8

In a really large ovenproof casserole dish, layer onions, celery, olives, stewing beef (each time sprinkling meat with vinegar and seasonings) and potatoes. Finish with a layer of potatoes, pour over stock and cook, covered, at 170°C (325°F) mark 3 for about $2^1/2$ hr until the meat is tender.

OLD SUSSEX POTATO AND CHEESE CAKES

350g (12 oz.) cooked potato, mashed
pinch salt
25g (1 oz.) butter
50g (2 oz.) mature Cheddar cheese, grated
50g (2 oz.) plain flour, sifted
5ml (1 level tsp) dry mustard
1 egg, beaten

Put all the ingredients into a basin and beat thoroughly. Drop the mixture in spoonfuls on a lightly greased griddle or frying pan, flatten slightly and cook over a gentle heat, turning once, until lightly browned – about 10 min. Alternatively, bake at 200°C (400°F) mark 6 for 10-15 mins on greased baking sheets.

Sussex Pond Pudding

The name of this rich but delicious dessert is thought to have originated from the fact that you used a pound of every main ingredient. Most old Sussex puddings were cooked in a cloth, not a basin.

225g (8 oz.) self-raising flour, sifted
100g (4 oz.) fresh white breadcrumbs
225g (8 oz.) butchers' suet, grated
2.5ml (2 level tsp) salt
75ml (5 tbsp) each milk and water,
approx. 100g (4 oz.) currants
175g (6 oz.) butter, softened
175g (6 oz.) dark soft brown sugar
grated rind 1 large lemon
Serves 6

Mix flour, breadcrumbs, suet and salt together and combine with water and milk to a soft, manageable dough. Divide the mixture into two (two-thirds and one-third) and roll each piece into rounds about 1cm (2 in.) thick. Press 50g (2 oz.) currants into the larger round and use to line a 1.1-litre (2-pint) capacity greased pudding basin, currant side down. Cream the butter and sugar together; beat in lemon rind and remaining currants. Place in the centre of the pudding. Top with smaller round of pastry, damp edges and seal well together. Cover with pleated greased greaseproof paper and kitchen foil. Secure with string and cook for about 2 hr in covered pan of boiling water coming half-way up the basin. Turn out to serve.

Pippin Pye

Golden pippins were so highly thought of that some were wrapped in silver paper and sent to Catherine the Great. The apples in this pie are left whole.

225g (8 oz.) shortcrust pastry (225g (8 oz.) flour, etc.)
6 pippins – large, juicy eating apples
12 cloves
1 small stick cinnamon
pared rind 2 orange
50g (2 oz.) butter
25g (1 oz.) butter, melted
25g (1 oz.) caster sugar
Serves 6

Prepare the pastry, keep on one side. Peel and core the apples and put in a piedish in which they fit exactly; place a pie funnel in the middle, if necessary. Add the cloves, cinnamon and orange rind and dot the apples with butter. Roll out the pastry and use to cover the apples. Bake at 190°C (375°F) mark 5 for 25 min. Remove from the oven and brush with melted butter, sprinkle with sugar and return to the oven to brown.

SUSSEX PLUM HEAVIES

These were said to be carried by the shepherds and woodsmen in their pockets.

225g (8 oz.) self-raising flour
pinch salt
pinch ground cinnamon
75g (3 oz.) lard
75g (3 oz.) margarine
100g (4 oz.) currants
50g (2 oz.) soft brown sugar
about 120ml (8 tbsp) milk
beaten egg to glaze
Makes about 10

Sift flour, salt and cinnamon into a basin. Blend the fats together and add one quarter to the flour. Rub fat inro mixture. Add currants and sugar and mix to a soft manageable consistency with milk. Knead dough lightly on a floured board and roll out to an oblong about 30.5cm by 10cm (12 in. by 4 in.). Mark the dough into three and flake one third of remaining fat over two-thirds of the dough. Fold and roll to original size. Repeat twice more until the fat has all been used up. Leave to rest in the refrigerator for 1 hr. Roll dough 5mm (4 in.) thick and stamp out 5-cm (2-in.) rounds. Remove a 1-cm (^{1}/2 in) round from the centre of each. Put on lightly greased baking sheet, brush with beaten egg and bake at 230°C (450°F) mark 8 for about 7 min., then reduce to 190°C (375°F) mark 5 for a further 5 min. Eat on day of making.

RIPE TART

Here a crusty almond topping cloaks a filling of canned black cherries in a pastry case. In season, fresh juicy ripe fruit makes this taste even better.

225g (8 oz.) plain flour
pinch salt 25g (1 oz.) cornflour
10ml (2 level tsp) icing sugar
125g (4 oz.) lard and margarine, mixed
1 egg yolk
439g (15 oz.) can pitted black cherries, drained
100g (4 oz.) icing sugar, sifted
75g (3 oz.) ground almonds
2 eggs, beaten
few drops almond essence
Serves 8

Sift flour, salt, cornflour and icing sugar into a basin. Rub in the fats until mixture resembles fine crumbs. Add egg yolk and bind to a manageable dough with about 30ml (2 tbsp) coid water. Lightly knead the pastry on a floured board and use to line a 24-cm (9^1/2-in.) French fluted flan ring. Bake "blind" for 15 min. Arrange cherries in flan case. Beat together remaining ingredi ents and pour over cherries. Return to the oven at 170°C (325°F) mark 3 for 50-60 min. until firm and golden brown. Serve warm or cold.